Caste and Class in Industrial Organisation

A Case Study of Two Industrial Units in Tamil Nadu

G. Karunanithi

Commonwealth Publishers
NEW DELHI-110002
(INDIA)

The publication has been financially supported by the Indian Council of Social Science Research, New Delhi, and the responsibility of the facts stated, opinions expressed and conclusions reached is entirely that of the author and I.C.S.S.R. accepts no responsibility for them.

I.C.S.S.R. Consultant
Prof. Victor S.D'Souza

Published by

COMMONWEALTH PUBLISHERS

4378/4B, GALI MURARI LAL
ANSARI ROAD, NEW DELHI-110002
INDIA

First Published, 1991

ISBN 81-7169-142-0

CASTE AND CLASS IN INDUSTRIAL ORGANISATION

Printed at

Gaurav Printers
Maujpur
Delhi-110053

Foreword

The work Caste and Class in Industrial Organisation is a rewritten version of the doctoral thesis prepared with a specific focus on industrial relations in two factories located in South Tamilnadu.

The social relations in South Tamilnadu particularly in erstwhile Madurai and Ramnad Districts [now consisting of Madurai, Dindigul Quaid-E-Milleth (Anna), Ramanathapuram and Pasumpon Thevar Thirumagan Districts] have been characterised by strong bonds of kinship and caste identity [reaching fanatical limits]. This is also the location where traditional rivalries between Thevars [a backward group of peasants] and Pallans [an untouchable caste] were demonstrated through caste riots marked by violence ending in murders.

Madurai city, the historical capital of Pandian Kingdom has been the headquarters for both Ramnad and Madurai districts until about 1989. This city has been one of the earliest centres of textile industry and had its own dose of Marxism. The Communist Party of India and CPI [M] have been quite active among the proletariat particularly among the industrial proletariat and more specifically the textile labourers.

Over the decades after independence both caste and class formations showed their mutual strength and influence in different historical situations especially during elections. In the same period literacy levels increased from 47% in 1951 to 64% in 1990 in Tamilnadu. Education believed to be a liberating force would have enabled the younger generation to come out of traditional identities on caste and to have increased faith in class identities. This expectation is supported by the fact that both the successors of the Indian National Congress and the burgeoning backward classes movement [marked by the rise of DMK to political power succeeded by

AIADMK] would have influenced the people to come away from caste identities with lessened kinship ties and familial bondage. A verification of this academic expectation has been attempted in this research work.

The study reveals that caste identities do exist in proletarian environment and sometimes have overriding influence even in contexts where class identities become essential or crucial. However it fails to explain in clear terms as to why such conditions do exist? Is it due to 'false consciousness' or lack of consciousness? If it is 'false consciousness' how it is generated and sustained? If it is total lack of consciousness why such a lack? Of course there are some indications that management induced caste identities characteristed by management supported leadership, caste based recruitment to labour force, kinship ties of trade union leaders and so on that contribute to the perpetuation of caste identities.

The study is not an attempt to seek the answer or of all possible answers for the questions but understanding of the economic situation in terms of labour size, unemployment, alternative sources, agricultural employment and the impact of Dravidian movement on the question of caste and class. To what extent the various forms of culture reflected in its art, literature and architecture punctuated with fairs and festivals have encouraged/influenced 'false consciousness'.

However the study merits careful scrutiny as it opens up the problems of understanding caste-class dichotomy in Asian societies. Whether Weberian explanation is valid or Marxian interpretation is meaningful are points considered in this study. The author's careful handling of this problem adds a dimension to the study of class in India and I am sure scholarly circles would welcome this work and take further the vexed question of caste and class in India to a meaningful end.

Madurai
15.5.91

R. VENKATARATNAM

Acknowledgements

This work is an outcome of my doctoral thesis. The revision of the thesis for publication was undertaken in the year 1989 at the kind suggestion of my learned guide, Professor R. Venkatratnam, Head of the Department of Sociology, Madurai Kamaraj University, Madurai. He has been a constant source of inspiration to complete this work. His encouragement and unfailing help have kept me in a state of zeal, without which it would have been difficult to complete the work. I owe a debt of gratitude to him for his kind guidance throughout the venture.

I am thankful to Professor C.N. Natarajan, Professor A. Venkatesan and Professor V. Sankarasubramanian for their kind help in several ways to complete the work.

I am grateful to Professor Andre Beteille who has provided helpful comments and also made kind suggestions to improve my work. I am also grateful to Professor T.K. Oommen. Professor C. Rajagopalan and Victor S.D' Souza for their suggestions to add clarity in certain areas of my work. In fact their suggestions have helped me immensely to develop the work and to bring it to its present form.

I extend my thanks to the Indian Council of Social Science Research, New Delhi for having provided me with a grant to publish my work. I also express my thanks to the University Grants Commission, New Delhi for having given me an opportunity to engage myself in revising my thesis in the Departments of Sociology, University of Delhi and Jawaharlal Nehru University, under the scheme of visiting associateship.

I thank Mr. V. Ganesan, M.A., M. Phil., for his help in carefully proof-reading this work. My thanks are due to the Commonwealth Publishers, New Delhi for their excellent and prompt service in bringing out this volume in a nice get-up.

Finally I would like to place on record my appreciation to my wife, Malli without whose co-operation and sacrifice it would have been impossible to complete the work.

G. KARUNANITHI

List of Tables

List of Figures

Contents

1

Introduction

What we mean in modern terminology by industry is mechanised and technology-oriented production. Its basis is naturally mass and large scale production. The term "Industrial Revolution" refers to the beginning in England of the invention and the use of machines to simplify and multiply production of things that conventionally exploited natural resources and the human hands. It was a revolution because it shifted the basis of production from men to machines. The change in the mode of production and consequently in the organisation of production and distribution changed the face of all commercial undertakings. This led to changes in social and political structures as well. The struggle for capturing markets in the world involved England in a race with other European powers. It was in this effort that England consolidated her hold over India and made India one of her colonies. In course of time, the cottage industries of India readily succumbed to better organised British industry.

Industrialization in the early days encouraged private enterprise. The *laissez-faire* policy of England encouraged private enterprise. Unchecked freedom for entrepreneurs led to various problems like wages at subsistence levels, growth and perpetuation of slums, corruption of the natural landscape, and many other human problems. These gave rise to serious thinking on the basis of social organisation, the making and passing on of wealth from generation to generation and the protection of society's interest from the onslaught of personal gains and selfishness. This thinking in due course led to the abandonment of *laissez-faire* and unfair treatment of industrial workers—in other words, introduction of governmental control over the means of production. This in recent times has developed into the social control over industries.

The world over, industry has two main modes of organisation: one the open acknowledgement of the capitalist entrepreneur, and the other, the social or communal possesion of the means of production. In India, as elsewhere, the early days of industry were the heyday of private enterprise. But socialistic thought has penetrated modern Indian thought deeply and so modern Indian industry is greatly influenced by government policies and ownership. The joint sector, a combination of private and public ownership, is quite in evidence in the business map of India.

Development of Industries in India

Since independence, India has been making a determined effort to industrialize. In the modern times, power in the world community is closely connected with industrial process. This is one reason why India is committed to rapid industrialization. India's modern industrial thrust has other aims also—industries provide great employment opportunities for millions of people; they lead them to better standards of life and prosperity. Thus, India's present industrial policy is an integration of commercial realities and social responsibilities. And it may be stated that this is a universal modern trend.

The first large scale industry in India was cotton textile industry. It was started in Calcutta in 1818. But the real beginning of this type of industry was made in Bombay in 1854 with predominantly Indian capital and enterprise. In course of time, various types of large scale industry—jute, metallurgical, engineering, food, chemical, paper, glass and the like—were established in different places of India. However, in the initial period of industrialization, progress was exceedingly slow and irregular.

In the later part of the nineteenth century, the development of coal mines inspired the growth of various manufacturing industries in India. Towards the end of the nineteenth century, a number of paper mills were started. In the early part of the twentieth century, the swadeshi movement influenced industrial development to a great extent. However, a new era in the industrial history of India began with the establishment of the Tata Iron and Steel Company Limited at Sakchi (now Jamshedpur) in 1907.

The First World War (1914-1918) gave an impetus to industrial development in India. On the eve of the war, cement and sugar industries were started. But, at the same time, Indian industries suffered considerably because the import of machinery, spare parts and chemicals was curtailed due to shipping shortage. Thus, India could not set itself firmly on the road to industrialization till the end of the First World War. A few industries which developed during the post-war years (after 1918) either stagnated or decayed as they could not face foreign competition. Nevertheless, the growth of sugar, cement and engineering industries was notable. Similarly, considerable increase in the production of matches, glass, vanaspati and soap was noticed in this period.

The Second World War (1939-1945) also stimulated the development of Indian industries. Several new industries came into existence. Manufacturing machine tools and simple machinery, cutlery and pharmaceuticals was also introduced. In the post-war period (after 1945), there was a marked development of industries such as ball and roller bearings, carding engines, ring frames and locomotives. Other industries producing fertilizer, cement, sheet glass, caustic soda and sulphuric acid were also expanded during this period.

After independence, in the First Five-Year Plan (1951-1956), more importance was given to agriculture, irrigation and power than to industries and minerals. However, it set a comparatively modest target for new investments in industries.

But in the Second Plan (1956-61) and the Third Plan (1961-1966), the main emphasis was laid on producer goods industries with a view to attain self-sufficiency along with industrial progress. As a result, the progress in growth and production of industries was considerably high in this period. Especially, the Third Plan gave importance to machine-building programmes. After this, during the period of the Annual Plan (1966-1968), the rate of industrial growth slowed down.[1]

In spite of strong emphasis on industrial development in the Fourth Plan (1969-1974), industrial production slumped as against the targeted growth rate. In the Fifth Plan (1974-1979) and in the Sixth Plan (1980-1985), great importance was given to the growth and production of industries. But the rate of growth of industrial production was not up to the targeted level.

Whatever may be the rate of industrial production, India has been experiencing rapid industrialization. Every year new industries are coming up and not only getting expanded but also modernised due to innovation. The table given below shows the growth of India's industries in general.

Table 1

Industries by Decades

Year	*No. of industries*	
	All India	*Tamilnadu*
1961	9,161	805
1971	16,923	1,617
1981	1,05,037	9,833

Sources: (i) Annual Survey of Industries 1961-71 and 1981-82.
(ii) Statistical Hand Book, Tamilnadu, 1983.

It is seen that the rates of increase in industries all over India and Tamilnadu are more or less same.

1. This section owes much to M.R. Chaudhuri. M.R. Chaudhuri, *Indian Industries Development and Location* (Calcutta : Oxford University Press, 1970), pp. 1-18 and 153-155.

Textile industry has always held its own among India's traditional occupations. It languished with the entry of British textile industry into India. But the gradual spread of knowledge and expertise in modern industrial techniques, indigenous effort in the field got a new stimulus. The Indian Cotton Mills' Federation Report sums up the progress of this industry thus :

> The cotton textile industry (of the modern type) is the forerunner of India's transformation from an agrarian economy to industrial advancement. It laid the foundation for the development of a number of allied industries and services. The Indian entrepreneurship had its training ground in textile manufacture and the subsequent proliferation into manifold avenues of industrial progress and economic activity had been made possible by the pioneering efforts of the textile industry.[2]

The decade-wise growth of cotton textile mills in India is shown in the table given below.

Table 2

Cotton Textile Mills by Decades

Year	*No. of cotton textile mills in India* *Spinning mills*	*Composite mills*	*Total*
1951	103	275	378
1961	192	287	479
1971	373	291	664
1981-82	442	281	723

Sources; Indian Textile Bulletin 26 (1980) and 29 (1983).

Though industry is spread all over India, its concentration is in Bombay. Commercial and geographical factors are

2. *Report of the Expert Committee on a Framework for the New Textile Policy*, Kanthikumar R. Podar, Chairman (New Delhi : Government Press, 1984), p. 3.

responsible for this. The city's dominance in the business world attracts rich and enterprising entrepreneurs to it. Raw material and good transportation facility are easily accessible. Also the city's humid climate is ideal for this industry.

There are two types of cotton mills. One is the spinning mill which spins the yarn used to make cloth. The other is the composite mill which does both spinning and weaving. The former is predominant in the south and the latter in the north. In the southern states, textile industry, especially spinning, has developed considerably along with industries. In Tamilnadu, there are more spinning mills than in other southern states. This may be accounted for by the development of handloom and powerloom industries in the state. Though a number of new mills have been started all over the state in recent times, the development of the cotton spinning and weaving mills in the state is primarily the result of British initiative. Two spinning mills are selected for the present study.

Thus Tamilnadu and other states of India are getting industrialized in varying degrees. Industrialisation has made the transition from a traditional way of life to a modern way, a momentous experience. Life in an industrialized society is greatly different from life in a traditional society. Theorists of industrial society like Inkeles and Kerr confirm that the logic of industrialism transcends cultural barriers. As a result, industrialized societies move rapidly away from traditions.[3] Yet the pace of modernization depends upon the hold which tradition has on the country. In nations like India, tradition in terms of caste, family, marriage and the like is deep-rooted, and gives way to change at a slow pace. But European nations have proved much more susceptible to changes in the framework of society. This is one reason as

3. A. Inkeles, "Industrial Man : The relation of Status to Experience, Perception and Value," pp. 1-31 and C. Kerr et al., *Industrialism and Industrial Man : The Problems of Labour and Management in Economic Growth*, pp. 170-172 as cited by Uma Ramaswamy, "Tradition and Change among Industrial Workers," *Economic and Political Weekly* 14 (February 1979) ; 367-376.

to why the progress towards modernization in India is not as rapid as in the European countries.

Impact of Industrialization on Caste System

Still, notable changes are taking place in caste system and other social institutions in India. These changes are mostly brought about by industrialization. Since the present study includes caste and its role in industry as one of the main aspects, it is relevant in this context to discuss the impact of industrialization on caste, the predominant system of social stratification in India.

In the pre-industrialization period, caste had been an extraordinarily intricate and relatively inflexible form of stratification. It tended to resist changes. Nevertheless, it allowed status mobility for exceptional cases. It was, thus, considered more or less a closed system. But in the recent decades, caste system is undergoing changes more rapidly than it did in all its earlier history. However, these changes cannot be described as fundamental; they are only peripheral.

In modern India, industrialization creates opportunities for large scale employment. It lends its way to occupational mobility. This benefits talented individuals from different social strata. This enables them to secure a better livelihood and to move to higher status. Consequently, caste system faces the challenge of modernity.

Industry, generally, does not provide scope for the formation of caste-based relationship among its employers and employees. In other words, it is case-blind. It brings together persons from different castes. In terms of their relationship within the industry, these persons cannot observe their traditional social norms relating to caste. Presumably industrial organisations provide the development of work ethos in which the workers work together, dine together and move freely with one another without inhibitions. Especially the caste inhibitions are ignored, though not completely suspended, in the interactions among the workers. Kuthiala observes:

In the factory situation, the Harijans, as untouchables,

are relatively unknown. They are treated merely as members of the working class and traditional religious taboos on caste relations are ignored.[4]

By and large, industries throw their doors open to people of all castes who are ready to avail themselves of the opportunities. The so-called low castes, especially the Harijans, also find scope for employment in industries by which they move to higher status. The development of industries has thus provided scope for upward mobility for all the low castes. It remains to be seen how far the dynamics of change minimizes the functions of caste and change the core of its structure.

In this context, we may refer to the idea of Marx. He writes: "Modern industry, resulting from the railway system, dissolves the hereditary divisions of labour, upon which rest the Indian castes, those decisive impediments to Indian progress and Indian power."[5] Marx suggests that industrialization will generate forces that will break down the caste barriers. He sees no need for special efforts or planning to eradicate castes; all that is required is planning for rapid industrialization.

Kingsley Davis observes that if industrialization proceeds rapidly in India, the caste system will certainly disappear by the end of this century.[6] Castes will disappear sooner or later provided that industrialization in India spreads at a faster rate than till now.

However, more than a century has passed since Marx made the prediction. Yet India is not free from the hold of caste system. The view of Kingsley Davis has also not come true, though a rapidly industrialising India is close to the twenty-first century. Perhaps, India is yet to be industrialized to the degree envisaged by Marx and Kingsley Davis.

4. S.K. Kuthiala, *From Tradition to Modernity* (New Delhi : Abhinav Publications, 1973), p. 138.
5. Karl Marx and Frederik Engles, *On Colonialism* (Moscow : Progress, 1968), p. 85.
6. Kingsley Davis, *The Population of India and Pakistan* (Princeton : Princeton University Press, 1951), pp. 73-74.

Nevertheless, it cannot be denied that industrialization has brought about some change in the caste system, especially in its periphery. At the same time, it has narrowed down the yawning gap between the high and the low castes.

The view that class distinctions emerge as a result of changes taking place in caste system is supported by some scholars in contemporary times. For instance, Beteille[7] and Anil Bhatt[8] believe that caste in India is slowly giving way to class. Similarly, D'Souza[9] and Holmstorm[10] say that caste is being replaced by class. But some scholars in early twentieth century maintain that caste system is stable and at times it even reinforces itself. For instance, Senart,[11] Hutton[12] and Furnivall[13] hold that caste continues to exist in India. Pocock feels that in urban areas, the development of caste system is complete.[14]

But neither of the views on caste system is fully true of contemporary India. In other words, caste has neither become weak nor has it found full expression. Certain peripheral changes are taking place in case system. Mukerjee, who is more or less of the opinion that changes have been marginal and limited in range, writes:

The caste system tolerated novelties and protected its

7. Andre Beteille, *Caste, Class and Power : Changing Patterns of Stratification in a Tanjore Village* (Berkeley : University of California Press, 1965), p. 4.
8. Anil Bhatt, *Caste, Class and Politics* (Delhi : Manohar, 1975), pp. 198-199.
9. Victor D'Souza, "Caste and Class : A Reinterpretation," *Journal of Asian and African Studies* 2 (1967) : 192-211.
10. Mark Holmstorm, "Caste and Status in an Indian City," *Economic and Political Weekly* 7 (April 1972) : 769-774.
11. Emile Senart, *Caste in India : Facts and the System*, trans. S. Denison Ross (London : Methun, 1930), p. 152.
12. J.H. Hutton, *Caste in India*, 4th ed. (Bombay : Oxford University Press, 1963), pp. 111-132.
13. J S. Furnivall, *Netherlands, India . A Study of Plural Economy*, p. 464 as quoted in K.L. Sharma, *Essays in Social Stratification* (Jaipur : Rawat, 1980), p. 4.
14. David F. Pocock, "Sociologies : Urban and Rural," *Contributions to Indian Sociology* 4 (1960) : 63-81.

essence from them. The changes have been confined to the politico-economic domain only.[15]

Caste continues to exist in India with its core elements. It also assumes new functions in accordance with changing social situations because of its adaptive or resilient nature. A similar view is held by Ghurye,[16] Srinivas[17] and Gould.[18]

Caste, thus, seems to be an indestructible element in Indian life, and capable of adjusting to new situation. The remarkable thing to note here is that caste is a force that cuts across religions. People belonging to one religion have deserted it to join some other religion, but yet maintain their identity in their new religion as they belong to particulr castes. The reality of this continuing force of caste is also seen in the caste consideration that influences political choices in India.

However, the formation of a "working class" as a category in industrial societies in contemporary India is evident. This gives rise to a new situation in which caste and class co-exist. As Yogendra Singh points out, class incorporates some of the elements of caste.[19] Similarly Sharma observes: "Caste and class are inextricably tied together and predominance of the values of caste suppresses considerably the expression of class consciousness".[20] Therefore, classes have not yet crystallised in India as castes are. Castes tend, even now to be resilient to challenging situation and try to preserve their core in this complex society. Hence the

15. Ramakrishna Mukerjee, *The Dynamics of Rural Society : A Study of the Economic Stracture in Bengal Villages* (Berlin : Academic Verlag, 1957), p. 6).
16. G.S. Ghurye, *Caste ond Race in India*, 5th ed. (Bombay : Popular Prakashan, 1969), pp. 1-28.
17. M.N. Srinivas, *Social Change in Modern India* (Bombay : Allied, 1966), pp. 89-117.
18. Harold A. Gould, "Towards a 'Jati' Model for Indian Politics," *Economic and Political Weekly* 4 (February 1969) : 291-297.
19. Yogendra Singh, "The Changing Pattern of Social Stratification", in *Dimensions of Social Change*, ed. M.N. Srinivas, S. Seshaiah and V.S. Parthasarathy (Bombay: Allied, 1977), p. 152.
20. Sharma, *Social Stratification*, pp. 56-61.

attempt to study the caste and class relationship in industrial organisations.

There are a number of research studies dealing with industrial relations, labour problems, industrial absenteeism, trade unions, industrial disputes and other related aspects. The present study confines itself to caste and class relations in certain areas of two spinning mills situated in Madurai District. A comparison is also made between these mills in terms of caste and class relations. It is important to mention that only limited research studies have so far been made on this aspect. So, an empirical study of this sort in this area is justified. This study is more comprehensive than other related studies. It surveys a wide area of caste and class relationship in the two spinning mills. The following objectives have been set forth for the study:

(i) To find out to what extent caste and class relations are significant in the matter of selection and promotion of workers and staff in the mills;
(ii) to find out the polarization of workers and staff towards caste and class relations in interacting situations in the mills; and
(iii) to find out the influence of caste and class relations in trade unions in the mills.

Area of Study

In pursuance of these objectives, the investigator has chosen two spinning mills in Madurai District.

Madurai District has been selected for this purpose for many reasons. It is slowly but steadily getting industrialised. Some of the factors favouring the growth of industries in this district are the availability of (i) entrepreneurs with modern ideas, (ii) labour capable of picking up skill in a short period and (iii) agricultural produce such as sugarcane, groundnut, cotton, etc.[21] The district has industrial estates at Madurai,

21. *Scope for small scale Industries in Tamil Nadu: A Study by Government of India* (Madras: Tamil Nadu Small Industries Development Corporation Ltd., 1971), p. 77.

Thirumangalam, Theni and Dindigul.[22] It also has an estate for food-and-fruit-based industries at Batlagundu, a small town close to Madurai City. It occupies the sixth place as far as industrial development in Tamil Nadu is concerned.

The industrial history of Madurai District is closely linked with the textile industry. It is, as a matter of fact, one of the textile centres of South India. It retains the second place in the matter of concentration of cotton textile mills in Tamil Nadu. Coimbatore, the major centre of cotton textile mills in Tamil Nadu as well as South India, occupies the first place. But textile mills in Madurai District were famous even before modern industrialization. A few of its spinning or textile mills have long been popular and famous. Besides, the spinning mills in the district is increasing in number every year and also getting modernized in an admirable way. The number of spinning mills has increased from two in 1921 to fourteen in 1981.

And finally, this district is a familiar place to the investigator who is acquainted with officials occupying key posts in a few mills in and around Madurai City. Their willingness to help him in conducting this research was an inspiration to him.

For the present study, two mills were selected on the basis of purposive sampling method. They are not similar in size and produce.[23] Their time of establishment is different. They work under different ownership patterns—one under the private sector and the other under the co-operative sector. They are situated in different backgrounds, that is, urban and rural. These factors were also taken into consideration for selecting the mills as the study involves a comparison of these two along caste and class lines.

22. In 1986, the Madurai District was bifurcated into two: One is Madurai District with Madurai as headquarters and another is Anna District with Dindigul as headquarters.
23. Mill A has 25,000 spindles, whereas there are one lakh spindles in mill B. Mill A is concentrating only on spinning but mill B, which is a composite mill, does both spinning and weaving. However, the present study has been restricted to spinning unit for the sake of uniformity.

Mill A, which is small in size and concentrating only on spinning was established in 1965. It is a co-operative concern and is situated in a village close to its taluk headquarters (Melur) which is about 25 kms. to the north of Madurai City. Its situation is typically rural. On the other hand, mill B, which is big in size and concentrating both on spinning and weaving, was established in 1923. It is a private concern situated in the southern part of Madurai City. In this mill, only spinning unit was taken for the uniformity.

The study was conducted in three stages. The first and preliminary stage was carried out between April and June 1980, the second stage was done between May and June 1981, and the third between May and June 1983. During the preliminary stage, a detailed interview was conducted with a limited number of workers, trade union leaders, and a few office staff in order to get a general idea about certain specific aspects of the mills. In addition to this, observation was also made to note certain vital issues, such as caste or class consideration among workers during interacting situations, influence of caste or class on union elections and caste conflicts. Based on the information collected through interview and observation, an interview-schedule was carefully prepared. At this stage, acquaintance with most of the employees from the factory side and with a few administrative staff was established so that the second stage could move smoothly. During the second stage, the respondents selected as sample of the study were interviewed carefully and intensively. The information obtained was noted against respective questions in the interview-schedule while interviewing the respondents. At the last stage, that is, at the time of data processing, the investigator revisited the two mills to fill up the gaps in information in the data collected.

SAMPLE

After acquiring adequate knowledge of the various aspects of the mills, the sample size was fixed. The total population of the two mills (975 in mill A and 1517 in mill B) was divided into three class categories—workers, operatives[24] and office staff—on the basis of occupation. Again they were divided into different groups on the basis of caste. Samples were drawn from each caste grouping of workers, operatives and office staff on the basis of stratified random sampling with proportional allocation. The sample size of 250 was arrived at by drawing ten per cent sample from each caste group. Tippet's Table was used to select the random samples. The sample consists of 233 workers (92 workers from mill A and 141 workers from mill B) and seventeen office staff (six staff from mill A and eleven staff from mill B). In addition to this, each trade union leader was interviewed elaborately in order to collect information pertaining to trade unions. However, they were not treated as samples but as resource persons.

TOOLS OF DATA-COLLECTION

Interview-schedule

The interview-schedule was administered in order to collect data from the respondents of the mills because an overwhelming majority of workers (an average of 81.48 per cent) drawn into the sample belonged to low educational category which refers to school education up to IX Standard. Normally workers, unless they complete high school education, are not able to furnish the required information if a questionnaire is used. So the interview-schedule was decided on for data-collection.

The interview-schedule was constructed in such a way as to be applicable to the workers, operatives and office staff. Another interview-schedule was constructed exclusively to collect data from the union leaders.

Participant Observation

In spite of the careful administration of the interview-schedule, relevant data for certain aspects could not be

24. The term "operatives" refers to maistrys, fitters, oilers, turners, welders, carpenters and electricians. They are also included in worker category.

collected. For instance, it was rather difficult to collect information regarding the influence of caste on union elections Generally, the respondents do not acknowledge that they prefer a man of their own caste as president or secretary of their union, irrespective of his qualities and qualifications. In such circumstances, the observation technique was of great use.

During the time of data-collection in the field, the investigator slowly gained confidence of the worker and the staff of the mills. After establishing rapport with them, he used to spend a few hours with everybody in the time office and also in the main office of the two mills to observe the interaction between the workers and the staff. He also attended a few union meetings to observe the discussions of the union members with their leaders. At the time of data-collection, he had the chance to observe union elections conducted by two powerful unions of mill A. Further, he observed the discussions of workers especially during lunch time. The observations were "participant" in the sense that the investigator could observe the discussions of the workers, union leaders and office staff in different situations inside the mill campus without involving himself in the work carried out by them. It was also "participant" in the sense the investigator mingled with a few workers in tea-stalls opposite to the main entrance of the two mills. Besides, he had a number of chances to be in company with some other workers who, during night time, were resting in the verandah of the main office building of mill A where he was provided with accommodation for the whole period of data-collection. The frequency and the intensity of contacts resulted in the break-down of communication barriers to the extent that the respondents began to treat the investigator as one among them.

He also had the chance to be with almost all the staff of the factory office and with a few of the staff of the main office as he spent most of his time inside the factory especially in the staff dining room where he conducted interviews with a majority of respondents. During the closing minutes of each shift as well as the beginning of every shift, he was asked to rest as the workers were then very busy with their work, checking and setting their machines. During such hours, he engaged himself in discussions with the factory and main office staff and also with the labour welfare officer without disturbing their work. He joined some of the factory staff for meals in the after-noons and nights, and moved freely with them in order to learn various aspects of the working of the mills. Especially, during night shift, the time office staff, after completing their routine work, engaged in conversation to while away the time without falling asleep. The investigator without any reservation participated in such discussions partly relating to mill matters as he had also spent some sleepless nights to interview the night shift workers. Sometimes, he was able to elicit information from them regarding certain aspects like caste association, staff selection, labour recruitment and groupism among staff. At the end of each day, these discussions and observations were carefully recorded in detail.

In this study, both qualitative and quantitative analysis were made. Generally, the qualitative data were converted into percentages. Chi-square test (non-parametric test) was used for most of the tables consisting of qualitative data in order to test whether the attributes—two or more—taken for analysis are associated or not. For quantitative data such as age and income of the respondents, student's t-test was used to test the difference between the means of the two samples drawn from mill A and mill B.

Limitation

This study covers employees of four different categories: workers, operatives, office staff and union leaders. It has limited its scope to the study of caste and class in recruitment and promotion of employees, their interacting situations and their unions. But it does not study the caste and class in social life of the employees, that is, the community life in their residential areas because of space and time factors. It has also limited its area to industry, specifically to two spinning mills in Madurai District. The reason for this has been explained earlier in this chapter.

The order of the chapters is as follows. In Chapter III, socio-demographic particulars of the employees have been discussed. The understanding of such particulars would provide the context in which the caste and class identities of the employees in various situations can be studied. Chapter IV deals with the importance of caste and class in recruitment and promotion of the employee. Chapter V discusses the polarization of employees towards caste and class in different interacting situations. In Chapter VI, caste and class relations in trade unions are explained. The last chapter summarizes the important findings of the study.

2

Caste and Class : Conceptual Analysis

Caste and class are two different principles of social stratification. Caste, an age-old social institution, is entwined with the life of Indians. One's position, high or low, in the social hierarchy is invariably decided by one's birth. On the other hand, class refers essentially to differences in life standards caused by economic factors. It is now slowly emerging in India as a system of social stratification. A wealthy person who belongs to the lowest caste in the traditional framework can now identify himself with the upper class. In modern India, thus, a peculiar situation does come into being as a result of contradictory economic and power interests of various groups. Nevertheless, caste still remains the basic and dominant criterion of social stratification.

Caste

The English word 'caste', according to Dumont, has been derived from the root words *casta* (Portuguese) and *castus* (Spanish). The former refers to something not mixed, a pure breed, and the latter signifies chastity. The word 'Caste' seems to have been used in the sense of race by the Spanicards, and to have been applied to India by the Portuguese in the middle of the fifteenth century.[1]

Caste, according to Burnouf, is constituted by the elements : "the division of functions, the hereditary transmission of these functions and hierarchy."[2] Bougle also acknowledges the last two features specified by Burnouf. Bougle does not treat "the division of functions" as a key factor in the caste system. Instead he brings in the idea of the "reciprocal repulsion". Other scholars have rarely touched upon this aspect. Different groups in society, according to Bougle, repel rather than attract one another; each group retires within itself, isolates itself, makes every effort to prevent its members from contracting alliances or even from entering into relations with neighbouring groups. Further he notes that these three aspects of caste system rest on the opposition of pure and impure.[3] This picture of a severe compartmentalization of the caste groups is not acknowledged by present-day scholars.

Guizot emphasizes heredity as the essential characteristic of caste system. He writes :

> Caste . . . is essentially hereditary; it is the transmission of the same situation and potentialities from father to son. Where there is no heredity, there is no caste.[4]

Blunt's statement of caste system is in agreement with the observations of many others. He, after analysing the definition of caste system by Gait, has carefully elaborated it in this way :

> A caste is an endogamous group, or collection of

1. Louis Dumont, *Homo Hierarchicus : The Caste System and Its Implications* (London : Weidenfeld and Nicolson, 1970), p. 21.
2. Burnouf, *Essai sur le Veda, ou etude sur les religions, la Litterature et la constitution sociale de l' Inde*, p. 218, as quoted in C. Bougle, *Essays on the Caste System, trans.* D.F. Pocock (Cambridge : Cambridge University Press, 1971), p. 10.
3. Bougle, *Caste System*, p. 27.
4. "Le Civilisationen Europe," p. 138, as quoted in C. Bougle, *Caste System*, p. 9.

endogamous groups, bearing a common name, membership of which is hereditary, arising from birth alone; imposing on its members certain restrictions in the matter of social intercourse; either

(i) following a common traditional occupation, or
(ii) claiming a common origin, or
(iii) both following such occupation and claiming such origin; and generally regarded as forming a single homogeneous community.[5]

Senart holds the idea that castes are, generally, conceived as a political system as against the observations of others that caste is a social institution. Taking the structuralistic stand. he defines caste thus :

A caste system is one whereby a society is divided up into a number of self-contained and completely segregated units (castes), the mutual relations between which are ritually determined by a graded scale.[6]

Bailey's definition of caste system in India refers to three characteristics—its "rigidity", and its ramifications in cultural and structural terms.[7] The first definition speaks of the ascription of social status and its immutability. This idea is more or less similar to that of Weber, Senart, O'Malley, and Mayer. Bailey is convinced of the viewpoint that regidity as the essential feature of the caste system is beyond criticism. Howver, castes are no longer a closed system. In modern times, they have been experiencing at least peripheral changes.

Bailey goes on to say that the second definition relating to the Indian set of religious beliefs is the cultural type which

5. E.A.H. Blunt, *The Caste System of Northern India* (London : Oxford University Press, 1931), p. 5.
6. Emile Senart, *Caste in India : Facts and the System*, trans. S. Denison Ross (London : Methuen, 1930), p. 35.
7. F.G. Bailey, "closed Social Stratification in India," *European Journal of Sociology* 4 (1963) : 107-123.

is more relevant than the first since the caste system has been defined in terms of religious beliefs or ideas connected with purity. He notes that in the purity-impurity opposition, the three principles of caste system—hereditary specialization, hierarchy and opposition of parts—are implied. He also sees that the purity-impurity formula has provided a satisfactory definition of caste system. Thus the caste system in India is a system of religious beliefs. The third definition of caste by Bailey is a structural definition based on exclusiveness, exhaustiveness and ranking of caste system.

Though Bailey, Sharma comments, has attempted to formulate a "compromised definition" of caste system by including cultural and structural aspects, he remains basically a "culturalist" and does not become a "structuralist". The reason is that he has not emphasized the study of the relations between the higher and the lower castes in any specific situation which becomes the criterion for determining caste structure.[8]

While referring to cultural and structural definitions of caste, Yogendra Singh raises two issues : (i) whether caste as a structural phenomenon is supposed to be particularistic and Indian in substance or has it universal properties? and (ii) as a cultural reality whether it belongs primarily to the Indian tradition or whether it crosses beyond Indian boundaries and has a universalistic form. On the basis of these two principles Singh outlines four types of caste principle : (i) cultural universalistic : it is considered as a matter of ideology or value system, particularly that of hierarchy. Weber and Ghurye hold this idea as they think caste-like cultural bases of stratification could be found in most traditional societies; (ii) cultural particularistic : it is the ideology of purity-pollution which refers to India alone. Dumont and Srinivas have the same view; (iii) structural universalistic : it considers caste only as a particular case of general phenomenon of a closed form of social stratification and (iv) structural particularistic : it confines itself to Indian society.[9]

8. Sharma, *Essays on Social Stratification*, p. 8.
9. Yogendra Singh, "Sociology of Social Stratification," A Trend Report in *A Survey of Research in Sociology and Social Anthropology*, 3 Vols. (Bombay : Popular Prakashan, 1974) 1 : 311-382.

It is evident from this analysis that endogamy, hierarchy, heredity, and traditional occupation are essential features of caste system. All these features are discussed by other scholars like Weber,[10] Hutton,[11] Beteille,[12] Srinivas,[13] Ghurye,[14] Mandelbaum[15] and Senart.[16] However, caste has close relationship with purity-pollution concepts and rituals. This relationship has been explained by Bailey,[17] Weber,[18] Mandelbaum,[19] Dube,[20] Kathleen Gough,[21] Mackim Marriott,[22] Mayer,[23] Srinivas[24] and Dumont and Pocock.[25]

Caste stratifies Indian society into a number of segments. This stratification involves the unequal distribution of rights and privileges among the people. The rights and privileges determine their status. As a result, inequality—high or low,

10. Max Weber, *From Max Weber : Easays in Sociology*, trans. and ed., H.H. Gerth and C.W. Mills (London : Routledge and Kegan Paul, 1948), pp. 396-409.
11. Hutton, *Caste in India*, pp. 46-70.
12. Beteille, *Caste, Class and Power*, p. 46.
13. Srinivas, *Social Change*, p. 3.
14. Ghurye, *Caste and Race*, pp. 1-28.
15. David G. Mandelbaum, *Society in India*, 2 vols. (Bombay : Popular Prakashan, 1972), Vol. 1, pp.14-15.
16. Emile Senart, *Caste in India: The Facts and the System* (New Delhi: Ess Ess Publications, 1975), pp. 1-38.
17. Bailey, *Closed Social Stratification in India*," pp. 107-123.
18. Weber, *From Max Weber*, p. 123.
19. Mandelbaum, *Society in India*, Vol. 1, pp. 192-205.
20. S.C. Dube, "Cultural Factors in Rural Development," *The Jouraal of Asian Studies* 16 (1956) : 19-30.
21. Kathleen Gough, "Caste in Tanjore Village," in *Aspects of Caste in South India, Ceylon and North West Pakistan*, ed. E.R. Leaeh (Cambridge, 1962), p. 11.
22. Mackim Marriott, ed. "Little Communities in an Indigenous Civilization," in *Village India* : Studies in Little Community (Phoenix Books, 1969), p. 189.
23. Adrin C. Mayer, *Caste and Kinship in Central India* (Berkeley : University of California Press, 1973), p. 33.
24. M.N. Srinivas, *Religion and Society among the Coorgs of South India* (Oxford : Oxford University Press, 1952), p. 26.
25. Louis Dumont and David F. Pocock, "A.M. Hocart on Caste : Religion and Power," *Contributions to Indian Sociology* (1958), p. 47.

superior or inferior—comes into existence. The different groups of society, thus. are linked with one another by the relationship of superiority and subordination. Caste, no doubt, ranks the status of people and forms a hierarchy which becomes a social scale to place an individual or a group.

Dumont distinguishes between the gradations of caste and stratification. The gradations of caste, he says, are based on the ideology of the opposition between pure and impure derived from the Hindu religious values, whereas class stratification is bound up with the variables of economic and political power; that is, it seems from the opposition of superior and inferior. The former is designated as hierarchy and the latter as power. Hierarchy and power are independent of each other, although under certain conditions one may subsume the other.[26] Dumont, thus, gives separate meanings for the terms "caste gradation" and "stratification". He opposes the Anglo-American writers who look upon caste as a form of social stratification. He takes caste as an expression of hierarchy which is a consciously organised principle as against stratification which is a principle constructed by sociologists on the basis of variable criteria.

It is rather difficult to accept the view that caste system is only a hierarchy and not a stratification. It is a peculiar device stratifying the Indian population into different segments. This kind of stratification was mainly determined by birth, the core of caste system, in pre-Independent India. The same view is held by Smelser.[27]

Caste and Subcaste

In this scheme of stratification, it is pertinent to mention that caste is a larger unit and subcaste a smaller one, a part of the former. Both of them are endogamous and hierarchial in nature. But the specific rules of a subcaste are applicable to the members of that small unit only, whereas the rules of a caste are applicable to all the members of that large unit

26. Dumont, *Homo Hierarchicus*, pp. 65-78.
27. Neil J. Smelser, *The Sociology of Economic Life* (New Delhi : Prentice-Hall of India, 1965), p. 66.

irrespective of its divisions, the subcastes. However, there is a close relationship between these two. Mayer raises a question in this regard as to how we should relate the smaller and larger units. For, he points out, there are two approaches: one group of scholars feel that there is no essential difference between the two terms, whereas others use them for different kinds of groups.[28] The first approach is shown in Ketkar's statement:

> The words "caste" and "subcastes" are not absolute but comparative in signification. The larger group will be called a caste while the smaller group will be called a subcaste in comparison with smaller or larger.[29]

Mayer is also more or less of the view that the subcaste must be placed as part of the caste rather than as a separate entity. He, therefore, believes that the largest division within the caste is the subcaste which has enough properties common to the caste to be a caste-like unit.[30] The second approach is expressed, for instance, by Blunt who maintains that there is an essential difference in the way one subcaste or one caste is discreet from another. He, thus, writes that endogamy is not a rigid divider of subcastes to make them the same as castes. He also doubts the similarity in the attributes of smaller and larger bodies.[31]

Nevertheless, subcastes have the essence of the caste system. Therefore, they may be considered real units in the system. The views of Ghurye and Srinivas are also similar to this. The subcaste, Srinivas claims, is endogamous. It is, to some extent, ritually and juridically autonomous.[32] Ghurye also notes that there is ample reason why, to get a sociologically correct idea of the institution, we should recognize

28. Mayer, *Cast and Kinship*, p. 6.
29. S.V. Ketkar, *History of Caste in India*, Reprinted (Jaipur: Rawat. 1909), p. 15
30. Mayer, *Caste and Kinship*, pp. 6-7 and 152.
31. Blunt, *Caste System*, p. 7.
32. Srinivas, *Religion and Society among the Coorgs*, p. 24.

subcastes as "real" castes.[33] However, in the present study, caste is mainly involved in the analysis.

Class

The principal type of social stratification in the contemporary west is in the form of class. The term "Social class" means any division or portion of a population marked off from the rest by different criteria such as income, occupation, education, prestige or status. It is more or less a distinct category or group. Several scholars have attempted to explain this concept which is one of the most widely used ideas to understand social reality.

Marx considers class a mirror reflecting the totality of relations in every society. He views class as a social reality, an existing fact. Class for him is not defined in terms of work function, income, but rather by the relations it bears with the mode of production. The mode of production thus provides the basic conceptual framework. Within the economic relations, class relations are primarily defined by the social relations of production. His theory of social class is based on the dialectical approach which has later been followed by various scholars working on social stratification.

Bendix and Lipset note that history, from Marx's view point, may be divided into several periods such as primitive communism, slavery, feudalism and capitalism. Each period is characterized by a predominant mode of production which gives rise to class structure consisting of a ruling class and an oppressed class. The struggle between these classes determines social relations in society. The ruling class owns or controls not only the means or instruments of production but also the moral and intellectual life of people.[34] Hence Marx says: "The ruling ideas of a period have always been nothing but the ideas of (the) ruling class.[35] The other class comprising

33. Ghurye, *Caste and Race*, p. 20.
34. Reinhard Bendix and S.M. Lipset, ed., *Class, Status and Power* (London: Routledge and Kegan Paul, 1974), p, 6.
35. Karl Marx, *Manifest der Kommunistischen Partei*, p. 93 as quoted in R. Dahrendorf, *Class and Class Conflict in Industrial Society* (London: Routledge and Kegan Paul, 1959), p, 14.

of workers is not allowed to own the means of production. They produce goods which they do not own and of whose ultimate use they may be ignorant. They are isolated from the ruling class. Thus, in all societies, social structure is influenced and nominated by economic interests.

Large scale industry, Marx notes, brings together many groups of workers and unites them into definite class groups against the capitalists. The workers are already a class against capitalists, but not yet for themselves. In the struggle, the workers become united and constitute a class for themselves. The interests they depend on become class interests. Thus, according to Marx, classes are of two types: class-in-itself and class-for-itself.

For Marx, a class "in itself" is one in which the various strata, although engaged in dissimilar work, are united by their broad social and economic ties. They form a class objectively against capitalists, but remain unaware of their antagonistic relation with them. A class "for itself" is a class in which the members are very much aware of their objective antagonistic relations with the capitalists and thereby develop an awareness of class interests and action necessary to defend such interests.[36] Thus the objective understanding of the workers of their position in relation to capitalists and their subjective awareness of their freedom, of their predicament correspond with that of other workers and of the unjustifiable authority and power of the capitalists are the main components of the Marxian theory of class. To Marx, a class to be called a class must fulfil both these conditions. In other words, a class "in itself" would be a precondition to form a class "for itself". The combination of these two components creates class consciousness among the workers.

Marx points out that the modern proletariat is the first "underclass" to develop its own large scale organisations (trade unions) which foster class identification and class consciousness. The concept of class consciousness in Marxism does not correspond to the idea of the consciousness that

36. Karl Marx, *The Poverty of Philosophy* (Moscow: Progress Publishers, 1975), pp. 159-160.

individuals have of their class status. In Marxian view, a man is side to be class conscious when he is (i) rationally aware of his own class interest and identifies with them; (ii) aware of other class interests and rejects them as illegitimate; and (iii) aware of and ready to use collective political means to realize his class interest.

The nature of class situation, Marx explains, differs according to the forces of production. When the forces of production, for instance, change from one form to another, the composition of the members of the classes may also undergo change. That is, the exploiting class of the previous phase is replaced by another class. Accordingly, at one stage, an overwhelming majority of persons in capitalist societies would be reduced to wage labour, the proletariat. They would be able to overthrow the numerically dwindling capitalists. At this stage, private ownership of the means of production would be abolished. The proletariat, the majority ruling class, would establish a classless society. Marx, thus, believes that the fall of the bourgeoisie and the victory of the proletariat are equally inevitable.[37]

Marx also confirms that classes as such do not constitute themselves until as organised groups they participate in political conflicts. The classes are political groups which are united by a common interest. Therefore, he says: "The struggle between two classes is a political struggle".[38] To put it simply, Marx believes that political power and political struggle are a special form of class struggle. However, to him, the "political power" of classes arises from the "relations of production". The relations of production are the basis for constructing the social relations of human societies.

It is relevant here to refer to the comment of Swingewood on Marx's theory of class. He points out that Marx, in his other works, repudiates his own dichotomous class model discussed above. In the historical study, "The

37. Karl Marx and Frederick Engles, *Selected Workers* (Moscow: Progress Publishers, 1975), p. 46.

38. Karl Marx, *Das Elend der Philisophine*, New ed., p 187 as quoted in R. Dahrendorf, *Class and Class Conflict*, p. 16.

Eighteenth Brumaire of Louis Bonaparte," Marx distinguishes several classes: the financial bourgeoisie, industrial bourgeoisie, petit-bourgeoisie, proletariat, landlords and free farmers. In other studies of France and Germany, he notes bourgeoisie, petit-bourgeoisie, farmers, peasants, serfs, agricultural workers, lumpen proletariat and feudal lords. It is clear from this that Marx does not articulate a simple two-class model as a historical fact.[39]

Swingewood's comment on Marx's enumeration of classes is not valid. It is clear from the enumeration of various classes by Marx that he was well aware of the plurality of social groups. These groups are not reducible to two large groups: capitalists and wage earners. Nevertheless, he makes it clear that class must not be confused with ordinary groups. Social class implies consciousness of a community and desire for common action with a view to certain organisation of collectivity. With this understanding Marx identifies two classes because in capitalist society only two groups—the capitalist and the wage earners—can have contradictory images of what society should be. This seems to be the main reason as to why Marx in most of his writings analyses class system in terms of two classes.

Later, in his third volume of Capital, Marx distinguishes three classes relating to three sources of income: owners of labour power, owners of capital, and land-owners. Their respective sources of income are wage, profit and ground rent.[40] So salaried workers, capitalists and land owners form three classes in modern society based on the capitalistic mode of production. However, according to him, there would untimately be two classes: proletariat and bourgeoisie. The importance of the ground rent diminishes due to the wide spread of industrialization.

Marx emphasizes that class is structually heterogeneous and a cluster of groups sharing a similar work function, values, aspirations and interests. Though the groups in the

39. Alan Swingewood, *Marx and Modern Social Theory* (London: Macmillan, 1975), 116.
40. Karl Marx, *Capital,* 3 Vols. (Moscow: Progress Publishers, 1959), pp. 885-886.

cluster frequently differ among themselves with regard to certain specific issues, they are knit together by a common interest. The ruling class, for instance, is never a simple homogeneous whole but consists of contradictory elements such as the representatives of heavy as well as small industries and finance capitalists. In spite of this they are held together by one overriding interest, the exploitation of labour power. Similarly, in some of the sections, the working class may articulate a coherent revolutionary class consciousness, while other sections may develop ideologies which reflect ruling-class conceptions rather than genuine proletarian interests.

However, the industrial workers in India. according to Marxian view, are a "class in itself". But the emergence of class consciousness is mostly curtailed by caste rivalries among the workers. It is understood that primordial ties of caste play a major role in inhibiting the development of class consciousness among them. Even within unions which, according to Marx, promote a revolutionary class consciousness articulated by the workers, there are rivalries among dominant castes. Such caste rivalries thoroughly distrub labour union activities. It is noted that subterfuges and tactical devices are carried out to pull down persons from other castes from the leadership of a labour union.

Marx emphasizes that the working class is deemed to be a class only when it is organised for class action. However, in Indian industries, workers are not organised in unions for class action but mainly for protecting their jobs. The union leaders, instead of promoting class consciousness among the workers, become the supporters of the management. They, like maistrys, tend to be the custodians of the interests of the management and thereby tend to act against the class interests of labourers.

Another trend in India is multi-unionism in industries. Powerful unions which have cordial relationship with industrial management try to prevent other unions from sharing power with them. The result is inter-union conflicts. Thus, the inter-union and also intra-union conflicts in Indian industries are not at all in keeping with the ideas of Marx on working class. The class interests among the workers are, thus, inveigled by caste interests.

It is also relevant in this context to mention that the Marxian conception of social class may become real in societies only if the means of production are completely owned by capitalists. The capitalists' practice is to exploit labour in quest of more profits. But, in such societies, the rapid growth of public and joint sectors tends to reduce the tendency to split the populations into two hostile groups or classes—propertied and non-propertied. Therefore, in those societies including India, this type of classes which Marx contemplates may not be clearly identified or categorized.

Moreover, the history of industrialism shows that the human conscience and sense of social justice have also grown more sensitive with the progress of industrial capitalism. The end of the era of open market and the birth of the era of government control signifies this. Hence Marx's prediction of an end to the erstwhile social system is yet to become a reality.

Other definitions of class widely used in the west, and particularly in America, do not consider property as the only criterion of class. They include a number of criteria—economic and non-economic—to explain the formation of class. As far as India is concerned, it seems to be reasonable to consider this view for the purpose of class analysis. The criteria such as occupation, income and education are used to stratify the population of the two spinning mills (samples) in terms of class for analysis. Nevertheless, power conditioned by "status honour" seems to be a suitable criterion to stratify the population in India because of the reason that India is basically a caste-based society.

It is important to mention that an industrial organisation, like other bureaucratic organisations, is segmented in the form of hierarchy. For instance, the Board of Directors, members of the management, middle management and the workers are limbs of hierarchy. However, this segmentation in industry based on hierarchy is conducive to the smooth flow of power from the top echelon to the bottom. This power is mostly conditioned by status groups in the industrial organisations based on bureaucracy. The workers, by virtue of this bureaucratic structure, become powerless irrespective of their castes. This makes them feel that they belong to one class. This feeling which is experienced temporarily by the workers within the industry seems to disappear when they go back to their community life. This shows that they are still in the grip of caste. A similar trend is found among the nanagerial staff. Therefore, the class formed by the workers in modern industries is not the "class for itself" visualized by Marx.

The "middle class" mentioned by Marx is not a bourgeoisie stratum but rather a combination of technical professions such as bureaucrats and clerical staff. It is noted that none of them owns property, that is, means of production in the Marxian sense. Therefore, there is a notable change in the social structure of industrial society. Now, it is not relevant to regard class merely in terms of propertied and non-propertied people. Nevertheless, class can also be explained in terms of status ("prestige") and power. That is the reason why Weber's discussion on "multi-dismensional structure" embracing class, status and party is often cited as the basis of the modern stratification theory.

Weber refers essentially to distribution of power in the matter of social stratification. Power is the nucleus of the Weberian theory of stratification. He writes : "Power is the chance of man or of a number of men to realize their own will in a communal action even against the resistance of others who are participating in the action".[41] He mentions three different bases of power : classes, status groups and parties. The places of classes, status groups and parties are economic order, social order and legal order respectively. These three elements are the distribution of power within a community. Thus, Weber's idea of stratification centres round the unequal distribution of power.

Weber thinks that the divisions in society based on economically conditioned power are classes. Therefore, he shares, to a certain extent, the Marxian objective view on

41. Weber, *From Max Weber*, p. 180.

class and extends it by adding a subjective element in the form of status groups. To begin with, he is in agreement with Marx regarding property as a crucial factor. He writes :" 'property' and 'lack of property' are, therefore, the basis categories of all class situations."[42] He also notes that a "class situation" exists whenever men are similarly situated by their "relative control over goods and skill". This control produces income, procures them other goods, gains them a social position, and leads to a certain style of life. Thus, according to Weber, the ownership or non-ownership of material goods or of definite skills constitute the "class situation" which, to him, is ultimately "market situation". Further, he noted that those persons whose fate is not determined by chances of using goods or services for themselves on the market, do not constitute a class. Weber considers them "status group."[43]

Weber holds the view that classes are not communities, but "class situation" emerges only on the basis of communalization. The communal actions that directly determine the "class situation" of workers and entrepreneurs are the labour market, the commodities market and capitalistic enterprise.[44] This line of reasoning goes counter to Marx's assertion that classes are communal groups.

However, Weber contends that the Marxian model of class based on economic factor is inadequate to explain the complexity of stratification. Therefore, he introduces two other major bases of power. One is status groups and the other, parties. He observes : " 'Status' is a quality of 'social honour' or a lack of it and is . . . conditioned as well as expressed through a specific style of life."[45] Status groups are normally communities which are distinguished from classes. He considers caste a status group in which status distinctions are guaranteed not merely by conventions and laws but also by rituals.[46] The third major basis of power lies in parties.

42. Weber, *From Max Weber*, p. 182.
43. Ibid., p. 183.
44. Ibid., p. 185.
45. Ibid., p. 405.
46. Ibid., pp. 188-189.

Weber maintains that the three bases of power are independent of one another, although they may be related to one another. Thereby he rejects Marx's contention that social and political dimensions of power are ultimately dependent on economic dimensions. For Weber, the key source of power in modern society is to be found in bureaucracy but not in the ownership of the means of production. Therefore, he thinks that the increased complexity of modern industral society leads to the development of the vast bureaucracies that become increasingly interconnected and interdependent. He observes : "The actual social position of the official is normally highest . . . the official predominantly derives from socially and economically privileged strata because of the social distribution of power . . ."[47] Besides, he mentions that the officials must be trained experts. In the industrial bureaucracy of India, social status in terms of high or low caste is maintained in the staff recruitment. It is, therefore, no wonder to find that the managerial staff belong to high castes. This does not mean that there is no one from either low or scheduled castes. However, they are very few in number. Since the power conditioned by status honour (caste groups) seems to be more relevant than the other two, it is used to divide the population in any organisation in India based on bureaucratic model.

It is observed that, in earlier centuries, the status of a Hindu was undoubtedly assessed. In other words, his status was determined only by his birth. But, at present, status is achieved through several means such as education, occupation, income, power and social movements. For instance, a person in the lower rung of caste hierarchy, will try to move to a higher status by taking up a new occupation as against his traditional work. Industrialization and modern education are mainly responsible for such occupational mobility which results in status mobility.

Moreover, different movements in India seem to be an important means for status mobility. This is evidenced by backward class movements which aimed to achieve social

47. Weber, *From Max Weber*, p. 200.

status on par with other higher castes. Similarly, caste associations with political backing play their effective role not only in gaining status but also in achieving political power. Thus, the result may be the unequal distribution of power conditioned by "status honour".

Dahrendorf's thesis concerning social class is that the society has to be visualized in terms of the 'coercion' theory of social structure. In other words, 'change and conflict' have to be assumed as ubiquitous, all elements of social structure have to be related to instability and change, and unity and coherence have to be understood as resulting from coercion and constraint.[48] As a reaction to the 'economic determinism' of Marx and the deterministic claim of the 'functional' theory of stratification, Dahrendorf has provided this 'coercion' theory.

Dahrendorf's analysis of class is, more or less, based on Weberian model of authority. According to him, social conflicts would arise systematically among groups which differ with respect to authority they enjoy over others. Like Weber, he explains authority as a kind of power attached to social position. This power is legitimate in the sense that it is limited by social norms and supported by sanctions up to these limits. He says, therefore, that the essence of power is the control of sanctions. A group of people with power give orders and obtain what they want from others. The power formulates and upholds social norms in a society. The application of these norms of human behaviour in the form of sanctions necessarily creates a system of inequalities of rank. This stratification is therefore an immediate result of the control of social behaviour by positive and negative sanctions. For instance, in any society, norms define some characteristics as positive (such as being an aristocrat or having more education than average) and some other characteristics as negative. If people in the society do not conform to those positive characteristics, the norms entail discrimination against them. But those who conform to the norms are rewarded. This results in two opposite and conficiting groups in the society.

48. Dahrendorf, *Class and Class Conflict*, p. 237.

Thus the division between 'conformists' and 'deviants' constitutes an element of social inequality.

Dahrendorf uses the word 'conflict gropus' instead of classes. However, these groups are labelled as social classes—one is coercive and another is coerced. Such domination and subjugation are found in all areas of social life. These classes emerge out of the conditions of social structure. He defines class almost exclusively in terms of conflict : '.class is always a category for the purpose of the analysis of social conflict and its structural roots, and as such it has to be separated strictly for stratum as a category for purposes of describing hierarchical systems at a given point of time."[49] But this definition of class does not imply the existence of conflict as a necessary or continuous element in the relations between classes.

Dahrendorf's analysis of class in terms of conflict groups (power group and powerless group) may also be applied in a broader sense to stratify the industrial population of India. The power group in industrial organisations consists of the top executives like chairman or Managing Director and also other employees occupying various positions because they always safeguard the interest of the management. On the other hand, the powerless group includes the workers. This group, in various occasions, may not conform to the rules formulated by the management. Undoubtedly this confrontation would result in industrial conflict. This seems to support Marx's view that the conflict involves two hostile groups, but in Dahrendorf's analysis of class, the authority or power is the crucial divide.

The limited analysis of Marx, Weber and Dahrendorf in this chapter reveals that the Marxian dichotomy of clear cut classes—bourgeoisie and proletariat—and Dahrendorf's 'Coercion' theory (power group and powerless group) of social structure may be more applicable to the highly industrialized and capitalistic countries. But the Weberian model of social stratification, especially in terms of status groups (castes) is nearer the truth of the industrial condition in Madurai District of Tamil Nadu.

49. Dahrendorf, *Class and Class Conflict*, p.:76.

3

Socio-demographic Composition

This chapter deals with socio-demographic composition of the workers and staff in the mills. A study in terms of age, sex, marital status, rural-urban background, religion, caste, caste association, class, education, income and political affiliation of respondents and unions has been made with a view to find out variations among the respondents in the mills with regard to these variables. Such an understanding of the socio-demographic background will enable us to appreciate the caste and class identities of the respondents in various situations.

Age

There is difference in the distribution of respondents in mills A and B in the different age groups. This is shown in Table 3.

There is a small difference between mean ages of the respondents in the mills (39.72 in mill A and 37.15 in mill B). That is the reason why the age composition of them shows that a fairly high percentage (42 per cent) of the respondents belong to the age group 33-43. An overwhelming majority of the respondents in mill A (75.51 per cent) belong to this age group. In mill B, the majority (40.79 per cent) belong to the age group 22-32. It is evident from this that there are more young employees in mill B than in mill A. This may be explained in terms of the age of the two mills. Mill B is thrice as old as mill A (63 years and 21 years respectively). Therefore, in mill B, a generation of workers have retired leaving scope for young persons to enter the mill in recent times. On the other hand, mill Awhich is 21 years old, naturally consists of an overwhelming majority of middle aged employees who were recruited to service about a couple of decades back.

Table 3

Respondents by Age

Age Group	*Mill A*	*Mill B*	*Total*
22-32	17 (17.35)	62 (40.79)	79 (31.60)
33-43	74 (75.51)	31 (20.39)	105 (42.00)
44-54	6 (6.12)	44 (28 95)	50 (20.00)
55 and above	1 (1.02)	15 (9.87)	16 (6 40)
Total	98 (100.00)	152 (100.00)	250 (100.00)

Note : In this Table and also in subsequent Tables, figures within brackets represent percentages of the sample.

$t=2.5507$ $df=248$ $P<0.5$

In mill A, the female workers who were already employed only in reeling section, constitute less than two per cent of the total population of labour force. Since their numierical strength was negligible during preliminary study, they were not taken into consideration at the time of sample selection. But the question of sex ratio of the workers in mill B does not arise as it did not employ women for any job.

Marital Status

In both the mills, a high majority of the respondents (94.9 per cent in mill A and 84.87 per cent in mill B) are married. It is, however, found that the percentage of married respondents is higher in mill A than in mill B. This is mainly due to the reason that the percentage of young respondents in mill B is higher.

Rural-urban Background

The mills are situated in different backgrounds: mill A is established in a small village which is about 25 kms to the north of Madurai, whereas mill B is lacated in the southern part of Madurai City. This locational difference has its impact on the distribution of respondents with reference to rural and urban backgrounds.

Table 4

Respondents by Backgrounds

Background	*Mill A*	*Mill B*	*Total*
Rural	62 (63.27)	71 (46.71)	133 (53.20)
Urabn	36 (36.73)	81 (53.29)	117 (46.80)
Total	98 (100.00)	151 (100.00)	250 (100.00)

It is clear from the Table that a majority of the total respondents in mills A and B (53.2 per cent) come from the rural area. However, the percentage of respondents coming from rural areas is higher in mill A than in mill B. The reason is obvious: mill A is situated in a small village surrounded by a number of villages. Nevertheless, it is interesting to find that a fairly high percentage of respondents (46.71 per cent) in mill B also come from villages in spite of its location in Madurai City. The reason may be that there are a number of villages situated in the outskrits of the Madurai City. The villagers were attracted to mill jobs as there are ten mills—eight spinning mills and two composite mills—situated in and around the city. The villages are 2-10 kms from the mills. Therefore, the villagers in large number have joined the mill.

It is important to note that a fairly high percentage of respondents (36.73 per cent) in mill A are urban workers who come from Melur, one of the taluk headquarters of Madurai district. This is the only town for a number of surrounding villages within a radius of 15 kms. It is situated at a distance of 2 kms from the north of the mill. On the other hand, all the urban workers (53.29 per cent) in mill B come from various parts of Madurai City.

Religion

The respondents are distributed into three religious groups: Hindu, Muslim and Christian.

Table 5

Respondents by Religion

Religion	*Mill A*	*Mill B*	*Total*
Hindu	92 (93.88)	144 (94.74)	236 (94.40)
Muslim	2 (2.04)	3 (1.97)	5 (2.00)
Christian	4 (4.08)	5 (3.29)	9 (3.60)
Total	98 (100.00)	125 (100.00)	250 (100.00)

It is clear from the above Table that an overwhelming majority of the respondents (94.4 per cent) in both the mills are Hindus. The percentage of Muslim and Christian respondents is meagre. This is due to the fact that the Hindus in Madurai urban agglomeration as well as in Melur taluk constitute a large majority of the population. However, it is important to mention that the Muslims in Melur town constitute nearly 20 per cent of the population. In spite of this, the percentage of Muslims (2.04 per cent) in mill A is almost negligible. The reason is that the Muslims in the town are already engaged in agriculture and business. It is reported that they do not have the inclination to mill jobs.

Caste

Generally, there is a relationship between the increase in workforce and the differentiation in its caste composition. In other words, large diversification in the caste composition of workforce depends on the increase of workforce in industrial organisations. This is supported by Chitra Joshi in her study on textile workers in Kanpur [1] This trend is also reflected in the mills studied. The respondent in the mills are distributed in fifteen castes and the two faiths of Christianity and Islam.

It is important to mention that the caste distribution in the universe is reflected in the sample too as the sample is based on the stratification of mill population by occupation and caste, and proportionate allocation. In the sample of the two mills, the castes such as Mukkulathor, Naidu, Pillai and Scheduled Caste occupy the first four places in the caste order based on numerical strength of each caste. A brief discussion of these castes is relevant in this context.[2]

1. Chitra Joshi, "Kanpur Textile Labour, Some Structural Features of Formative Years", *Economic and Political Weekly* 16 (November 1981): 1823-1838.
2. The discussion regarding different castes much owes to *Census of India, 1961*; *Gazetteer of India: Tamil Nadu (Ramanthapuram District), 1972*; Somalay, *Madurai Maavattam* (Vedaraniam: K.G.K.G. Publication, 1980) and Edgar Thurston, *Caste and Tribes of Southern India*, 7 vols. (Madras: Government Press, 1909).

Table 6

Respondents by Caste

Caste	*Mill A*	*Mill B*	*Total*
Mukkulathor	25 (25.51)	58 (38.16)	83 (33.20)
Pillai	17 (17.35)	21 (13.81)	38 (15.20)
Naidu	7 (7.14)	26 (17.11)	33 (13.20)
Scheduled Caste	19 (19.39)	10 (6.58)	29 (11.60)
Other Castes	30 (30.61)	37 (24.34)	67 (26 80)
Total	98 (100.00)	152 (100.00)	250 (100.00)

Mukkulathor

This group of castes consists of three broader divisions: Kallar, Maravar and Agamudaiyar. All the three are collectively called Mukkulathor. They are included in the backward classes schedule. Kallars are mostly found in the distr cts of Madurai and Tanjore and also in the small principality of Pudukkottai. They extend somewhat into the districts of Kamarajar in the south and Trichy in the north.

There are differences between the Kallars in Madurai and Tanjore. The Kallars in Madurai remain independent in spirit, and those of Tanjore have been converted to more Brahmanic values. For instance, the women dress like their Vellala neighbours. The Tanjore Kallars who have become conformists, look with scorn their Madurai brothers whom they consider coarse and half-savage.

In Madurai district, there are two types of Kallars: The Ambalakkārars in the east including Melur taluk and the Pramalai Kallars in the west. The two areas are separated by Madurai city. Both divisions of them are engaged in agricultural operations.

Dumont, while referring to the psychological characteristics of the Pramalai Kallar, observes: "They are neither shy nor reserved, but have a direct and animated approach, a lively curiousity, a frankness which can easily appear as brutal or indiscreet".[3] He says that this is also true of the other Kallar and Maravar. In the pre-independence days, the Pramalai Kallars were treated as criminal tribe.[4]

The marital relationship of Kallars are not as strong as such relationship among other Caste-Hindus. The spouses are separated by a simple method called *Thirthukattuthal* (dissolving the marital relations). This term is generally but inappropriately translated as divorce. This act consists of giving a *turumbu* (a piece of paddy straw) together with betel and, possibly, payments to wife's brother by the husband. This must be done before witness and is accompanied by the declaration that he no longer has any connection with his wife, but only with his children. This practice is predominantly found among the Kallars in rural areas. Widow marriage is also practised by them.

The Maravars are predominant in the two taluks of Madurai district namely Thirumangalam and Usilampatti, and also in the districts of Tirunelveli, Ramnad and Pasumpon Muthuramalinga Thevar. They more or less resemble the Kallars in several respects with regard to social life. It is reported that they also have the practice of *Thirthukattuthal* and widow marriage. Especially Kondiyan Kottai Maravar were treated as criminals in the pre-independent period. They engage mostly in agricultural operations. Their general title is *Thevar*.

The Agamudaiyars live predominantly in the Sholavanthan taluk of Madurai district. They are also found in Ramnad and Tanjore and Nellai-Kattabomman districts. They

3. Louis Dumont, *A South Indian Sub-caste: Social Organisation and Religion of Pramalai Kallar* (Delhi: Oxford University Press, 1986), p. 24.

4. Ibid, pp. 26-32.

are said to be closely connected with the Maravars by descent. They also mostly resemble the Maravars in relation to appearance, habits and customs. But they do not follow the practice of *Thirthukattuthal* and widow marriage. Agriculture is their main stay. They are said to have been greatly influenced by the contact with Brahminism. They style themselves as Vellalas and Pillais and consider themselves superior to the other two divisions. Their general titular name is *Servai* or Servaikaran. The Kallars in mill A and Agamudaiyars in mill B are the predominant caste people. However, the broader category, 'Mukkulathor', has been referred to in the study.

Pillai

Several sub-castes of 'Vellālas' have the general titular name Pillai. They are described as "a peace-loving, frugal, and industrious people". They are basically cultivators. Some of them are land owners who employ low caste people for cultivation. They would not normally condescend to manual work. Some of them are well-educated, and employed in Government service and others are engaged in business. The Vellālas have four main divisions:

(i) Tondamandalam, or the residents of the Pallava country which includes the present Chingleput and North Arcot Ambedkar districts. The caste titles in this division are ***Mudali*, *Reddi*** and ***Nainar***;

(ii) Sozhia, or the dwellers of Chola country which includes the present Tanjore and Trichi districts. They have their caste title ***Pillai***;

(iii) Pāndya, or the inhabitants of the Pāndyan Kingdom of Madura and Tirunelveli. They also use the title ***Pillai***; and

(iv) Konga, or those who resided in the Konga country which corresponds to present Coimbatore and Salem. They are called ***Gounders***. However, the members of all these four major territorial divisions resemble one another in their essential customs. These divisions of Vellālas dine together, but they do not intermarry.

The members of the four divisions of Vellālas are further split into sub-divisions (having generally a territorial origin) and the members of which again do not intermarry. For instance, the Tondamandalam are sub-divided into the *Tuluvas* who are supposed to have come from the Tulu country; the Pundamalli Vellālas who are the residents of the town Pundamalli near Madras city; and the *Kondaikattis* who tie their hair in a knot without shaving it. None of these sub-divisions intermarry. The Sozhia Vellālas are sub-divided into the *Vellāan Chettis* (merchants); the *Kodikkāl Pillais* (betel growers); and the *Kānakkilināttārs* (the inhabitants of Kānakkilinādu). They do not normally intermarry. But the members in the unit have marital relationship with other sub-divisions. The Pāndya Vellālas are sub-divided into the *Kārkathas*, who are believed to be the inhabitants of a territorial sub-division called Kāraikādu; the *Nangudis* and *Panjais* whose origin is ambiguous; the Arumburs and *Sirukudis*, who are called so because they are from villages of those names in the Pāndya country; the *Agamudaiyans*, who are probably recruits from the caste of that name; the *Nīrpusis*, meaning the wearers of the sacred ashes; and the *Kottai Vellālas* or *fort Vellālas* who live with in a fort in Srivaiguntham; the Kongas are sub-divided into the Sendalais (red-headed men), Paditalais (leaders of armies), *Vellikkai* (the silver hands), *Pavalamkatti* (wearers of coral), *Malaiyadi* (foot of the hills), *Tollakādu* (ears with big holes), *Attangarais* (river bank), and others. The origin of them is not clearly known, but the members of which never intermarry.

The Vellālas in Trichy, Tanjore, Madurai and Tirunelveli districts have the general titular name Pillai. A section of the Pillais are vegetarians. Especially the Saiva Pillais are highly religious and pure vegetarians. Generally, they do not prefer occupations involving physical labour. They are, therefore, considered superior among the Pillais. But especially Kodikāl Pillai and Illathu Pillimār are non-vegetarians who go for manual work. They are included in the schedule of backward classes. Generally, the Pillais do not allow divorce and widow marriage. In the two mills taken for the study, those two divisions of Pillais are found in fairly large number. Nevertheless, the broader category 'Pillai' has been used in the study.

Naidus

The Naidu caste has three broad sub-divisions: Kammās, Balijās and Kavarais. The Kammās are considered migrants from Vijayanagar. They settled down in various parts of Tamilnadu during the time of the Vijayanagar kings. They are found in a few taluks of Madurai District such as Periakulam, Palani, Thirumangalam and Theni and in the south-eastern part of Madurai City. They style themselves Nāickers. They are a forward community.

The Balijā Naidus are believed to have migrated to Madurai from Andhra Pradesh during the Naicker rule in Madurai. They are mostly found in Srivilliputhur and Sattur taluks of the Kamarajar District. They are also found in Periyakulam, Vadakarai, Vedikapatti, Allinagaram, Kuruppatti and Thevaram in Madurai District. They are also included in the list of forward communities.

A section of the Naidu migrants in Tamilnadu call themselves Kavarais. They are included in the list of backward classes. They have marital relationship with the Balijās. But the Kammās do not have such relationship with either the Balijās or the Kavarais. However, all of them dine together and have certain common customs. The Kammās claim superiority over the other two divisions of Naidus because they are economically well to do. This may be the reason why only the Balijās and the Kavarais have joined the mills as workers. These three divisions of Naidus do not allow either divorce or widow marriage.

Scheduled Caste

The Paraiyars and the Pallars in Madurai District are the two major divisions of the scheduled castes. They are also known as Harijans, who constitute nearly one-seventh of the total population of Madurai District. Th :y are found in almost all areas of this district. They are predominantly agricultural labourers. Some of them who settled in urban areas for their employment move with Caste-Hindus apparently without inhibitions. But those in rural areas still have social and religious disabilities. They allow divorce and widow marriage. They are generally known as Harijans.[5]

The Mukkulathor respondents in both the mills constitute a fairly high percentage (25.51 per cent in mill A and 38.16 per cent in mill B) as they live in large numbers in the Madurai urban agglomeration (about 38 per cent) and in Melur Taluk (about 35 per cent).[6] Among the three divisions of the Mukkulathor respondents, the Kallars constitute a majority (66.67 per cent) in mill A and the Agamudaiyars (49.57 per cent) in mill B. The Kallars are predominant in Melur taluk and therefore their representation in the mill situated in that taluk is higher than that of the other two divisions. On the other hand, among the Mukkulathors, the Agamudaiyars are predominant in Madurai City and constitute a majority in mill B.

The Agamudaiyars are economically and educationally better off than the other two divisions of the Mukkulathors. This enabled them to migrate to Madurai City for their employment. In Ramnad District also the population of the Agamudaiyars in urban areas is higher than that of the other two divisions. It is inferred from this that the economic and educational development of a caste or subcaste mostly goes along with the spatial mobility of its members. It is supported by Beteille in his Tanjore study. He notes that the Brahmins, after disposing off their lands in villages, migrated to Madras and other big cities for their children's education and development.[7] Their native villages

5. The term "Harijan" which means "children of God" was introduced by Mahatma Gandhi to refer to Untouchables in India. But the Government of Tamil Nadu has issued orders calling them *Adi Dravidas*.
6. Information collected from *Madurai Corporation and Melur Taluk Office*.
7. Beteille, *Caste. Class and Power*. pp. 113-114.

which no longer met their growing needs did not provide opportunities for their educational and economic development.

In mill A, the Harijan, Pillai and Naidu respondents occupy second, third and fourth places respectively with regard to numerical strength. But in mill B, the condition is reverse as the Naidu, Pillai and Harijan respondents take second, third and fourth places respectively.

In Melur taluk, the Harijan population (about 16 per cent) is less than that of the Valaiyars (about 18 per cent) who are next to the Kallars in their numerical strength.[8] Like the Harijans, the Valaiyars are predominantly agricultural labourers, but they belong to the backward classes under Government classification. Though they occupy the second place in Melur taluk with regard to numerical strength, their population in mill is only two per cent. But the Harijan workers occupy the second place in numerical strength. The reason is that the mill authorities, as per the direction of the Tamil Nadu Government, employ 237 Sri Lanka Repatriates[9] as workers and out of them, a majority (51.26 per cent) belong to the scheduled castes. This addition to the already employed workforce of the Harijans has raised their numerical strength to the second place in the universe and hence a similar trend in the sample too. However, the population of the Harijans in the mill was higher than that of the Valaiyars even before the recruitment of the Sri Lankan Repatriates. They were given preference at the time of each recruitment through the Employment Exchange. Moreover, a considerable number of them were introduced by a Harijan Minister in the then Congress Ministry of Tamil Nadu.

The Pillai respondents occupy the third place in terms of their strength in the workforce in spite of their sparse

8. Data collected from the *Melur Taluk Office*.

9. The rehabilitation provided by the Government of India to the Sri Lanka Repatriates is generally in the form of resettlement in agricultural and non-agricultural operations. Some of them have been employed in industry. Almost all the Repatriates in Madurai area are employed in textile mills. A considerable number of them have taken a loan of Rs. 5,000 provided by the Government.

population (below 5 per cent) in Melur taluk.[10] This is mainly due to the reason that the first two chairmen of the mill belonged to the Pillai caste and they recruited their castemen who came from different areas of Madurai District as workers and clerks. This naturally improved their numerical strength and raised it to the third place.

The Naidus whose population in Melur Taluk is also meagre (below 5 per cent) when compared to other castes such as the Konar and the Moopanar (about 10 per cent each)[11] occupy the fourth place since they readily joined the mill in the initial period itself. Their interest in a job in the mill might have been doubled because of their castemen working in the mills in and around Madurai, serving as a reference group. The Naidu maistrys and politicians are also responsible for introducing some of their castemen into the mill.

As far as mill B is concerned, the Naidu respondents occupy the second place in spite of their low population (about 5 per cent) in the Madurai urban agglomeration.[12]

The Madura Coats is the first spinning mill started in Madurai in the year 1882. In the 1930s, S.R. Varadarajulu Naidu, who was a popular trade union leader from Salem, became familiar with the management of the mill. He introduced his castemen (Balijās) from Srivilliputhur, a town situated 55 kms to the south-west of Madurai City, as workers in the mill. In course of time, the Naidu workers brought their kinsmen and castemen for the mill jobs. This increased their population to a majority in the mill. More or less in the same period, a fairly large number of Naidus joined mill B as workers without recommendations as, at that time, mill jobs were not yet popular among other castes. This led to the chain migration of the Naidus from their native town seeking jobs in these mills. They settled down with their families in the neighbouring areas of the mills.[13]

10. Data collected from *Melur Taluk Office.*
11. Ibid.
12. Data collected from *Madurai Corporation.*
13. Information collected from a senior and knowledgeable maistry from the Naidu caste.

The Naidus in mill B constituted a majority of the workforce till 1960. After that, persons from other castes, especially the Mukkulathors and the Pillais joined the mill in large numbers. A majority of these Kukkulathors and Pillais are from neighbouring village of Madurai. A considerable number of them introduced their kinsmen and castemen in the mill as workers. After 1970, the Mukkulathor workers outnumbered the Naidu workers and now constitute a majority in the mill. Consequently, the Naidu workers came down to the second place in the caste order based on numerical strength.

It can be inferred from all these that mill workers introduce their own kinsmen and castemen as workers rather than men of other castes. This may be because of the obligation on their part to help men of their caste in securing employment. Srinivas supports this view:

> When a worker or white collar employee gets a job in town, he frequently becomes a source of employment for his relatives, caste-folk and other local people. This has happened in most if not all parts of India. . . .[14]

Though the Pillais constitute below 5 per cent of the population of Madurai City.[15] They occupy the third place in the workforce in terms of numbers. This is mainly because most of the early maistrys and a few staff in the mill were Pillais. They introduced their relatives and castemen in considerable numbers. At the same time, the mill management did not like the active participation of the Naidus in the Union organised by S.R. Varadarajulu Naidu. The Managing Director deliberately recruited the Pillais along with Mukkulathors in order to extinguish the domination of the Naidus. It is reported that workers belonging to these two castes were already in confrontation with the Naidu

14. M.N. Srinivas, "Social Environment and Management Responsibilities," *Economic and Political Weekly*, 10 (March 1975): 487-491.

15. Data collected from *Madurai Corporation.*

workers in the Madura Coats. It is, therefore, believed that the management was under the impression that the same trend would make its appearance in their mill too. This may be the reason why the management employed a large number of persons from the Pillai and Mukkulathor castes. This raised the Pillais to the third place with regard to the numerical strength.

The population of scheduled castes in Madurai District is 15.33 per cent as against 5.39 per cent in Madurai urban agglomeration.[16] The population of other castes such as the Sourashtras (about 30 per cent) and the Nadars (about 12 per cent) is higher than that of the scheduled castes in Madurai urban agglomeration.[17] In spite of this, the Harijan respondents occupy numerically the fourth place in the mill. This may be explained in terms of the purpose of the management in recruiting them. The Harijans are, by nature, submissive and do not involve themselves in strikes against the management.

Murphy's study supports this view. He finds that the Ādi-Drāvidas (scheduled castes) refused to support strikes organised by the Caste-Hindu workers of the Buckingham Mill in 1921. The reason was that they completely depended upon their wages for their survival. They were economically unable to sustain themselves during a strike so long or so much as the Caste-Hindus were able to do. They preferred to cast their lot with their employers to being with their colleagues who traditionally thought them inferior. Moreover, many Ādi-Drāvidas considered the British Administrators their protectors as they provided opportunities for their economic advancement which were denied to them by the Caste-Hindus.[18]

The Sourashtras who came from Sourashtra of Gujarat State are traditional weavers. They live in large numbers in

16. Census of India (*Primary Census Abstract*), 1981.

17. Data collected from *Madurai Corporation*.

18 E.D. Murphy, "Class and Community in India : The Madras Labour Union, 1918-1921," *The Indian Economic and Social History Review*, 14 (July-September 1977) : 291-321.

the central and eastern parts of Madurai. They constitute nearly one-third (about 4 lakhs) of the populalion of the Madurai urban agglomeration.[19] In spite of this, they are limited in number (5.33 per cent) in mill B. This has two explanations. Madurai is one of the centres for silk handlooms which provide jobs to hundreds of Sourashtras. Moreover, many of them are the owners of handlooms and their families as a whole engage in the process of producing silk fabrics. Familiar with the know-how of weaving silk fabrics, they want to monopolise this trade rather than to prefer mill jobs. A section of the Sourashtras are involved in trades mostly related to weaving, like selling dyeing materials, yarn, cloth and screen print. In addition to this, some of them are agriculturists and owners of small workshops manufacturing locks and iron-boxes. Nearly one-third of cinema theatres in Madurai City are owned by the Sourashtras. A section of the Sourashtras have, therefore, improved their economic position by their skilful and industrious nature.

Since a majority of the Sourashtras were employed and provided adequate provisions by a number of master weavers of their caste, they did not join the mill in large numbers. It is reported that they follow many of the rituals and customs of the Brahmins. They, therefore, claim to be equals of Brahmins. They support their claim by a *Sasana* issued by Queen Mangammal.[20] Hence they might have thought that becoming workers in a mill was infra dig to them. However, they are included in the list of backward classes.

But this evidence is not enough to explain why Sourashtras have not joined the mill in greater numbers despite the fact that they constitute a majority in the eastern and central parts of Madurai. Yet, they constitute a majority at the worker level in a mill situated in the outskirts of Madurai South run by a small group of Sourashtra entrepreneurs. This is, according to one of them, mainly due to their caste loyalties.

19. Data collected from *Madurai Corporation*.

20. *Gazetteer of India* : *Tamil Nadu* (*Ramanathapuram Distrct*), 1972, pp. 152-153.

Another important caste to be discussed here is that of the *Nattukottai Chettiyars* who are otherwise known as Nagarathars. They are categorised as one of a forward communities by the Government of Tamil Nadu. They are the traditional wealthy financiers of Tamil Nadu. They are often called the Marwaris of the South. Their traditional occupation till 1930 was moneylending and banking especially in South-East Asia and Ceylon. Jain describes them as the indigenous bankers of the South.[21] After that, they emerged as prominent industrialists in Tamil Nadu. They were in the textile industry even before 1930.

It is noted that only two workers in the sample are Nagarathars in spite of the fact that the mill was taken over in the early 1930s by a leading entrepreneur of that caste. The fact of the very limited population of the Nagarathars in Madurai City may not be the reason for this. But their disliking towards manual labour may be the reason. On the contrary, the Naidus who are also thinly scattered over Madurai City have joined the mill in large numbers. This is because of the reason that the Naidus, by nature, are hard workers and their economic background is not so sound as that of the Nagarathars.

In Table No. 6, the "other castes" consist of eleven castes and the two Faiths of Christianity and Islam. The castes included are : Konar, Chettiyar, Gounder, Asari, Valaiyar, Nadar, Mudaliar, Moopanar, Sourashtra, Velar and Reddiyar. The respondents from all these castes are working in mill A. But the castes such as the Gounder, Valaiyar and Moopanar are not in employment in mill B. Of all these castes, the Reddiyars and the Sourashtras constitute 6.58 per cent and 5.26 per cent of the respondents respectively in mill B, and respondents of the other castes in both the mills constitute below 5 per cent. It is found that neither of the mills has even one worker from the Brahmin community.

It is evident that except the Pillais and the Naidus, other high caste people seem reluctant to join the

21. L.C. Jain, *Indigenous Banking in India* (London : Macmillan, 1929), p. 45.

mills as workers. Therefore, the Mukkulathors who are considered lower caste people occupy the first place in both the mills in numerical strength. In other words, the Mukkulathors constitute one-third of the total sample size. On the other hand, the higher castes such as the Pillais and the Naidus in both the mills together constitute about one-fourth of the sample.

But studies on Indian workers show that factories always attract workers from all levels of traditional society.[22] A few of them are the Pune study by Lambert, the Kota study by Vaid and the Bombay study by Sharma. In Lambert's study, the two upper castes—the Brahmins and the Marathas—together constitute a majority of the Hindu workers.[23] Similarly, Vaid's study shows that more or less a majority of the Hindu workers belong to two upper castes.[24] In Sharma's study also, two-thirds of the Hindu workers belong to two upper castes.[25]

Considering the numerical strength of the staff it is found that the Pillais, Naidus and Kallars in mill A occupy the first three places respectively, whereas in mill B, the Sourashtras, Nagarathars, Pillais, Brahmins, Naidus and Agamudaiyars occupy the first six places respectively. Other castes are very thinly represented on the staff. It is noted that there is no Kallar on the staff of mill B. The reason for such caste distribution at the staff level is explained in the fourth chapter. However, the higher castes such as the Pillais, Naidus, Nagarathars and Brahmins constitute more or less a majority of the staff (49.18 per cent in mill A and 52.63 per cent in mill B) in the mills.

The Harijans do not find representation on the staff of mill B. But six out of the 61 staff in mill A are Harijans. Mill A comes under the co-operative sector and follows the staff selection procedure prescribed by the Government. So

22. Srinivas, *Social Change*, p. 64.
23. Richard D. Lambert, *Workers, Factories and Social change in India* (Princeton, N.J. : Princeton University Press, 1963), p. 3[illegible].
24. K.N. Vaid, *The New Worker* (Bombay : Asia, 1968), p. 41.
25. Baldev Raj Sharma, *The Indian Industrial Workers : Issues in Perspective* (Delhi : Vikas, 1974), p. 13.

these six Harijans were appointed on the basis of the reservation policy of the Government.

On the whole in mill A the Kallars and Pillais are the dominant castes. They are, at the same time, rivals. It was frequently observed by the investigator that the Kallars and the Pillais expressed their displeasure with each other with regard to certain matters. On the other hand, the Agamudaiyars and the Pillais are the dominant castes in mill B. Though the Naidus in this mill occupy the second place in terms of numerical strength, they are not able to dominate. This is mainly because of the recruitment of the Mukkulathors and the Pillais in large numbers.

Caste Associations

Caste associations are comparatively a modern phenomenon. They first emerged in the Nineteenth Century. They are voluntary organisations consisting of members of respective castes within a region. They give a new force to the caste system to play its role especially in the political area. Some caste associations actively participate in politics. They are able to solve a number of problems of the castes provided they are successful in politics. They also aim at the improving of social and economic status of their members. Most caste associations are thus organised around the general theme of promoting the welfare of an endogamous caste. They organise conferences to discuss various issues with regard to the development of the members of the respective castes.

Srinivas considers caste association an adaptive mechanism.[26] He feels that the desire for social mobility of a caste is expressed through the formation of caste sabhas. The formation of such sabhas results increasing the "horizontal stretch" of the caste.[27] Hardgrave also observes that the caste sabha represents an adaptive response of caste to social,

26. Srinivas, *Social Change*, p. 114.
27. M.N. Srinivas, *Caste in Modern India and other Essays* (Bombay : Asia, 1962), p. 98.

economic, and political changes.[28] Rudolph, however, suggests a more general process of adoption in order to bring about cultural mobility. He points out that caste associations facilitate change from macro-society to micro-society. He, while referring to Nadar caste, observes :

> Instead, they (the caste) seem, in good Hindu fashion, to have been reincarnated in a modern form as a caste association. It has become the vehicle for internal cultural reform and external social change. The caste association enables middle and lower castes to establish self-esteem under circumstances in which they had begun to feel the inferiority rather than the necessity of their condition and to win social esteem, first from the state, then the macro-society and last and more slowly from the micro-society of village and locality.[29]

Caste associations were formed in mill A during the time of data-collection. They are : the Muventhar Pannpatu Kazhagam (Mukkulathors), Tamizhvel Pannpattu Kazhagam (Pillais), Thirumalai Mannar Pannpattu Kazhagam (Naidus), Yadavar Sangam (Konars), and the Ambedkar Sangam (Harijans). A considerable percentage of the workers of these castes became their members. They pay annual subscriptions and mostly attend annual conferences organized by the main branches of the respective caste associations. The office bearers (President, Secretary and Treasurer) of these branch associations have frequent contacts with the main branches. They also receive periodical instructions from the main unit and act accordingly. Whenever their associations are in need of money, they collect funds by conducting cultural programmes.

It is learnt that in mill A the Muventhar Pannpattu Kazhagam covers about 60 per cent of the total population of the Mukkulathor workers; the Tamizhvel Pannpattu Kazhagam

28. R.L. Hardgrave (Jr.), *The Nadars of Tamil Nadu : The Political Culture of a Community in Change* (Bombay : Oxford University Press. 1969), p. 199.
29. Lloyd I. Rudolph and Susanne Hoeber Rudolph, *The Modernity of Tradition : The Democratic Incarnatlon of Caste in India* (Chicago, Illinois : The University of Chicago Press, 1965), p. 13.

covers nearly 45 per cent of the Pillais; Thirumalai Manner Pannpattu Kazhagam consists of about 30 per cent of the Naidus; Yadavar Sangam has about 40 per cent of the Konars and the Ambedkar Sangam has about 50 per cent of Harijans. It is clear that more than one-third of the employees from each of these castes have membership in their caste association. But such associations are absent in mill B. An average of twenty per cent of the Mukkulathor, Pillai Naidu and Harijan workers in the universe are members in their respective caste associations outside the mill. Similarly, workers from other castes such as the Nadars, Konars and Sourashtras constitute below ten per cent of the members in their respective caste associaions.

Caste association and labour union are antithetical. Caste association is an interesting mechanism developed mainly to preserve the core elements of caste against the process of modernization. It protects the interests of members in a caste. It also facilitates changes in their social, economical and political life. It never associates itself with another caste association because it aims to maintain its identity. It is, therefore, divisible force which intensifies the divisions of population in terms of caste groups.

On the other hand, labour union is an integrating force which unites the workers irrespective of their caste, racial or religious differences for a common cause. It works for the welfare of workers and their development at large. It is expected to promote class consciousness among the workers in order to make them aware of their position in relation to the capitalists, and their rights as workers. But the very purpose of the union has not been fulfilled because of caste loyalties and personal motives among the workers. So class consciousness amoag the workers is almost absent. Unless they have this consciousness they cannot form a "class for itself" in the Marxian point of view.

Further this can be supported by two case studies in mill A. One respondent who had been a union leader and is at present the secretary of the Mooventhur Pannpattu Kazhagam says :

> When I was the union secretary, I also had to attend to the caste association activities. As a Secretary of the association, I motivated some of the workers from my caste to become members of the association. I had to attend to the problems of my caste workers in the union without hesitation since a majority of them had membership in the association. Had I not considered my castemen with special care, I would have been blamed. Sometimes, I was not able to attend to the problems of my castemen because their problems as such were not genuine. In such circumstances, I lost the support of my castemen temporarily.

Another respondent who is a worker reports :

> Though the workers are in different unions, they get united by caste associations. For instance, if a Pillai contests for the secretary's post in one union, some of the Pillais in the other unions voluntarily work for his victory. A Pillai leader of one union will directly or indirectly help a Pillai in another union mainly because he belongs to his caste association.

It is inferred from this that caste loyalties strengthened by caste associations hinder the development of class consciousness among the workers and hence the impossibility of class crystallization.

Education

At present, the minimum qualifications prescribed for worker and staff in the mills are VIII standard (pass) and under-graduate (preferably B Com.) respectively. But, in the past, the management of the mills recruited persons with minimum literacy as workers and persons with S.S.L.C. (complete or incomplete) qualification as clerical staff.

The respondents in the mills are invariably literates. More than one-third (36.73 per cent in mill A and 38.82 per cent in mill B) of the respondents in each mill are in higher educational category including S.S.L.C., Technical course and

Degree course. However, a majority of the responeents (an average of 62.23 per cent) in both the mills belong to the lower educational category which refers to school education up to IX standard.

There is a relationshlp between educational qualification and caste status. This is shown in the Table given below:

Table 7

Education of Respondents by their Caste Status

Caste	*Mill A*		*Mill B*		*Total*	
	Lower	*Higher*	*Lower*	*Higher*	*Mill A*	*Mill B*
Mukkulathor	19	6	38	20	25	58
Pillai	9	8	11	10	17	21
Naidu	4	3	12	14	7	26
Scheduled Caste	10	9	9	1	19	10
Other Castes	20	10	23	14	30	37
Total	62 (63.27)	36 (36.73)	93 (61.18)	59 (38.82)	98 (100.00)	152 (100.00)

In mill A, among the Pillais, Naidus and Harijans (Scheduled Caste) the lower education group is almost balanced by the higher education group. But among the Mukkulathors and the "other castes", the lower education group is far larger than the higher education group. In mill B, the two categories are almost balanced among the Pillais and Naidus, whereas the lower education group far outnumbers the higher education group among the Mukkulathors and the Harijans. In both the mills, the "other castes" category may be ignored because it consists of too many castes to produce any significant result.

It is important to note that nearly half of the Harijan respondents in mill A belong to higher educational category. Of the total population of Harijans (188) in mill A, a majority

(58 per cent) consists of Sri Lanka Repatriates who have invariably completed high school education. Similarly, of the Mukkulathor respondents in mill A, nearly one-fourth have higher educational qualification, whereas in mill B, nearly two-thirds of them have higher educational qualification. However, the superior division among them, the Agamudaiyars, alone constitute an average of 71.21 per cent of highly educated persons, whereas the other divisions, the Kallars and the Maravars, collectively constitute 22.72 per cent. It has already been pointed out that the Agamudaiyars are educationally more advanced than the other two divisions of Mukkulathors.

Income

The following Table shows the income groups of the respondents.

Table 8

Respondents by Income

Income (Rs.)	*Mill A*	*Mill B*	*Total*
701—900	90 (91.84)	140 (92.11)	230 (92.00)
901—1100	4 (4 08)	5 (3.29)	9 (3.60)
1101—1300	2 (2.04)	3 (1.97)	5 (2.00)
1301—1500	2 (2.04)	4 (2.63)	6 (2.49)
Total	98 (100.00)	152 (100.00)	250 (100.00)

t=7.222 df=248 P = 0.5

In both the mills, a large majority of the respondents (91.84 per cent in mill A and 92.11 per cent in mill B) belong to the income group Rs. 701 to 900. The mean income of the respondents in mill A is Rs. 778.96 and in mill B is Rs 862.14. Hence there is relationship between the income of the respondents and their backgrounds.

Class

There are different indices used to stratify the population in terms of class categories. They ars: self-rating (that is, identification of a respondent with a social class by himself). income, occupation and education. These are the widely recognized indices of class categories. Of these, self-rating is usually considered a subjective index and the other three are called objective indices.

Occupation and income are closely related to each other and both are related to education. Since occupation includes both income and education, it it widely used as a measure of class. It is not only a source of income but an index and symbol of the style of life of the people and the level of prestige that is accorded to them by others. Lambert and Jaspal Singh[30] used occupation as the only criterion in their studies to classify industrial workers in terms of class categories. But, in this study, education, occupation and income are used to classify the responnents into different class categories. This is mainly because of the reason that the respondents belonging to different educational, occupational and income groups may identify themselves with others from similar groups.

It is clear from the table that there is a tripartite relationship among the variables—education, occupation and income. The level of income depends on the level of occupation and the level of occupation, in turn, depends on the level of education. In other words, the increase in the level of education results in the increase in the levels of occupation and income. Thus the education as an independent variable,

30. Jaspal Singh, "Trade Union Leaders: A study in Class Background and Social Mobility," *The Indian Journal of Social Work*, -2 (April 1971) : 63.

Table 9
Respondents by Class Categories

Occupational Group	*HIG*			*MIG*			*LIG*			*Total*
	SE	*TE*	*CE*	*SE*	*TE*	*CE*	*SE*	*TE*	*CE*	
HOG	2		9	2	—	4	–	—	—	17
MOG	—	—	—	2	14	—	—	—	—	16
LOG	—	—	—	7	—	—	207	1	2	217
Total	2	—	9	11	14	4	207	1	2	250

HOG : Higher occupational group (office state)
MOG : Middle occupational group (operatives)
LOG : Lower occupational group (workers)
HIG : Higher income group (Above Rs. 1200)
MIG : Middle income group (Rs. 1001-1200)
LIG : Lower income group (Below Rs. 1000)
SE : School education (up to SSLC)
TE : Technical education (Training or Diploma)
CE : College education (Under Graduate)

directly influences occupation and indirectly influences income too. This is represented in the following Figure.

Figure 1
Tripartite Relationship : Education, Occupation ann Income

Education

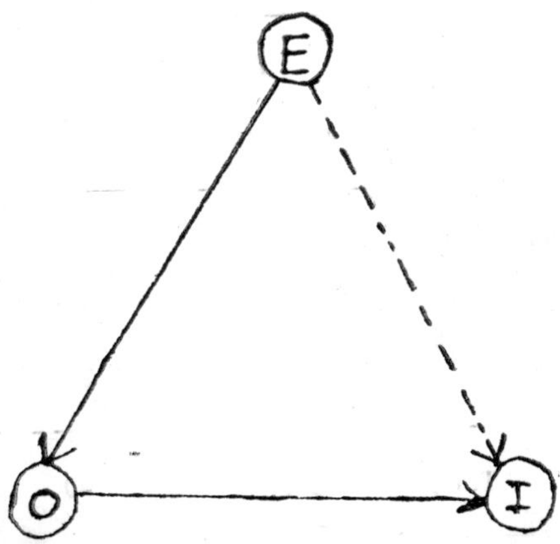

Occupation Income

This tripartite Relationship is statistically confirmed by chi-square test.

Table 10

Respondents by Education and Occupation

Education	*Occupation*		*Total*
	White-collar	*Blue-collar*	
Up to School education	4	216	220
Technical or College education	13	17	30
Total	17	233	250

$x^2=73.48$ df=1 P>0.001

Table 11

Respondents by Education and Income

Education	*Income (Rs.)*		*Total*
	Below 1000	*Above 1000*	
Up to school education	207	13	220
Technical or College education	3	27	30
Total	210	40	250

$x^2=138.9$ df=1 P>0.001

Tables 10 and 11 show that education influences occupation and income. In table 10, the operatives are also categorized as blue-collar workers as they are, by and large, engaged in manual work as their subordinates do. However, their position in mill A is ambiguous in the sense that they neither identify themselves with the workers nor the office staff. Thus they exist as a group distinct from their superiors and subordinates.

The operatives in the mill A think that they are vested with powers and privileges which the workers do not have. They, especially the maistrys, dictate, punish or even recommend the management to suspend or dismiss the erring workers. They have organised a union for themselves. They always protect the interest of the management within the social relations of production. They are, therefore, considered establishment-men.

On the contrary, ths position of operatives in mill B is different in the sense that they identify themselves with workers. It is supported by the fact that they do not havr separate union for themselves. Instead they have become members in different unions organised by the worker. Though they are considered establishment-men, they do not always protect the interests of the management. They support not only the genuine demands of the workers but to participate in strikes to achieve such demands. Though they wield their power over the workers, they still consider that they belong to the same cadre. For all practical purposes, they identify themselves with them. In other words, in this mill, they appear less as the establishment-men.

Whatever the power and privilege the operatives enjoy in the mills, they are not equal to the supervisors, their immediate heads. In other words, the supervisory cadre do not accept them as of their rank. They feel that they are above the operatives because they are possessed of technical qualifications like the diploma in textile techology. The operatives also know that they are below in rank to their supervisors, though their suggestions, in most of the time, form the basis of the decision of the supervisory staff. It because of such factors that Sheth sees in them the group that feels most deprived among the industrial worker-groups.

The socio-demographic profile of the respondents presented so far, constitute the base for analysing the caste, class relationship with respect to recruitment and promotion of the employees, their interacting situations and trade union activities. The recruitment and promotion of employees in terms of caste and class are discussed in the next chapter.

4

Recruitment and Promotion

The industries established in India during the second half of the nineteenth century and the early decades of this century were always faced with the problem of labour recruitment and labour discipline. Jobs in mills were considered degrading, especially by the high castes. Mill workers, Murphy notes, found it difficult to arrange the marriages of their sons and daughters. Gradually, however, prejudice wore off. Mill jobs provided regular, even if meagre, income. This was an added attraction to a rapidly growing population of the unemployed in our country. This development was congenial to entrepreneurs providing employment to the agricultural population who remained underemployed for several months in a year.

In the initial period, the managements of mills used informal ways to recruit workers. Murphy says that one of the familiar ways of recruiting workers was through the informal networks of communication mainly through workers already employed in them. An unemployed person would come to know about for opportunities in a mill through a kinsman who would be an employee in the mill or acquaintance there. He would approach an official at the mill gate for a job and provide his relative's name as a reference. It was, at that time, a usual practice for a manager or a time-keeper or a jobber (maistry) to wait outside the mill gate to invite workers to join the mill.[1] Kuthiala mentions another method—whenever a vacancy arose word was sent through workers to their kinsmen to secure the job.[2]

Murphy points out that at times of acute shortage of workforce the management would announce their need by tom-tom[3]—one of the traditional ways of spreading information—in surrounding villages. Sometime, the mill officials hired carts to tour neighbouring villages to pick up those who were in search of jobs. It was also a practice but rare to directly approach the mill owners related to them for jobs.[4]

In the first quarter of the twentieth century, the cotton mills in Bombay recruited workers through intermediaries or middlemen known locally as "jobbers".[5] Vaid mentions that they were in different parts of India known by different names such as "labour contractors", "sirdars", "mukkadams" and "kankanis".[6] They had vital role to play in the recruitment of workers throughout India in the early days. They often recruited workers at the mill gate. Sometimes, they went round neighbouring villages of the mills to recruit workers. From Murphy,[7] Myers,[8] Vaid,[9] Kuthiala[10] and Chitra Joshi,[11]

1. Eamn Mdrphy, *Unions in Conflict : A Comparative Study of Four South Indian Textile Centres, 1918-1939* (New Delhi : Manohar, 1981), pp. 32-34.
2. Kuthiala, *From Tradition to Modernity*, p. 118.
3. A person invariabiy from the Harijan community used to go around the streets beating a drum and making announcement regarding the vacant position in the mills.
4. Murphy, *Unions in Conflict*, p. 34.
5. K.N. Vaid, *Contract Labour in Manufacturing Industries, A Report and Analysis* (New Delhi : Sri Ram Centre for Industrial Relations and Human Resources, 1966), p. 73.
6. Ibid.
7. Murphy, *Unions in Conflict*, p. 35.
8. Charles A. Myers, *Labour Problems in the Industrialization of India* (Cambridge, Massachusetts : Harvard University Press, 1958), pp. 40-41.
9. K.N. Vaid, *Gheraos and Labour Unrest in West Bengal* (New Delhi : Sri Ram Centre for Industrial Relations and Human Resources, 1972), p. 142.
10. Kuthilala, *From Tradition to Modernity*, pp. 118-19.
11. Chitra Joshi, "Kanpur Textile Labour," pp. 1823-1838.

we learn that they recruited their kinsmen, castemen and friends from their own and surrounding villages. Crouch holds the view that the mill managements in Bombay left the task of managing the workforce in the hands of jobbers.[12] Usually jobbers recruited a gang of workers often from their villages and brought them to the mill and supervised their work. The workers' first loyalty was, therefore, to the jobbers and not to the mills.

Since the jobbers recruited their kinsmen, castemen and their villagers as workers, it might be that the workers were, in one way or another, known to each other even before recruitment. Vaid says that various departments in older mills could be identified in terms of caste, community, and native-village groups. The decision to join a union or to leave it, to support a particular demand, or to join a strike, was often made on social considerations in which the traditional pattern of relationship between villages or communities played dominant role.

It is clear that one of the major roles of the jobbers was to recruit workers for mill jobs. While discussing the functions of jobbers, Morais points out that their official work was largely technical and supervisory. They allotted work, granted leave and trained the workers. They also carried out minor repair to the machinery and enforced the company's work regulations. Since they kept the records of work load and attendance, they had to calculate the wages of all the workers. By and large, they acted as labour recruiters and supervisors.[13] They, according to Myers and Konnappan, enjoyed complete autonomy in the matter of recruitment.[14] They established, in one way or another, a vital link between the workers and the management. The perpetuation of this recruitment process relies not only on their ability to recruit a

12. Harold Crouch, *Trade Unions and Politics in India* (Bombay : Manaktalas, 1966) pp. 17-18.

13. Morris David Morris, *The Emergence of an Industrial Labour Force in India : A Study of Bombay Cotton Mills 1854-1947* (Berkeley, University of California Press, 1965), p. 142.

14. Charles A. Myers and S. Kannappan, *Industrial Relations In India* (Bombay : Asia, 1970), p. 96.

large number of workers but also on their ability to control them on the shop floor.

In the initial period of industrial establishment, the employers faced certain problems from workers. Vaid observes :

> Lack of labour mobility, low social status of factory work, caste and religious taboos, et cetera, were some of the problems with which most British employers and managers were not familiar and who felt ill-equipped to solve them. The gap was filled by the institution of middlemen who acted as recruiting agents for companies and also controlled labour.[15]

Generally, workers had to depend on the jobbers, to secure and retain their jobs. Workers expressed their gratitude through presents in cash or kind or even liquor. Murphy notes that a worker would, in special cases, present a cow or work in the jobber's house or field for nothing.[16] In many cases, Myers mentions, the jobbers were paid commissions by their employers for recruiting workers. Workers also had to pay "commissions" (bribes) to the jobbers to keep their job, get promoted, obtain leave or to be reemployed.[17] Radhakamal Mukerjee also observes : "...in Bombay, Ahmedabad, Kanpur, Nagpur and elsewhere, it is the system of recruitment by jobbers which has given rise to serious evils of bribery, corruption and favouritism which call for immediate remedy.[18]

Since Independence, the jobber system has been given up in almost all the industries. The recruitment of workers is done in different ways. But before going into this, we must deel with the motives of these workers for entering this field. The respondents gave three different reasons for taking so this job. These are shown in Table 12.

A large majority of the respondents (69.39 per cent) in

15. Vaid, *Contract Labour*, p. 73.
16. Murphy, *Unions in Conflict*. p. 35.
17. Myers, *Labour Problems*, p. 41.
18. Radhakmal Mukerjee, *The Indian Working Class* (Bombay : Hind Kitabs, 1945), p 30.

Table 12

Respondents by their Job Motivation

Casctes	*Decent Income*		*Advised by others*		*Accidental*		*Total*	
	A	*B*	*A*	*B*	*A*	*B*	*A*	*B*
Mukkulathor	13	23	8	30	4	5	25	58
Pillai	11	7	3	13	3	1	17	21
Naidu	5	12	2	13	—	1	7	26
Scheduled Caste	16	8	2	1	1	1	19	10
Other Castes	23	16	3	19	4	2	30	37
Total	68 (69.39)	66 (43.42)	18 (18.37)	76 (50.00)	12 (12.24)	10 (6.58)	98 (100.00)	152 (100.00)

Note: A and B refer to mill A and mill B respectively.

mill A say that they preferred the job because it provides a decent income, but a majoriiy of the respondents (50 per cent) in mill B report that they preferred the job because of the advice of their kinsmen and castemen, wishing to secure better living. Mill B which was established earlier than mill A recruited those who readily came forward to take mill jobs. In other words, the mill opened its doors to men of all castes irrespective of their age, skill, literacy and other factors. After joining the mill, the workers and the staff advised their kinsmen and castemen to join the mill. Most of the staff in the sample (five in mill A and seven in mill B) preferred the job because it provides a decent income.

The respondents in both the mills have secured their jobs in different ways. In the initial period of mill B, the maistrys (jobbers) played an important role in the recruitment of workers. They went round the neighbouring villages to pick up unemployed persons. They brought in mostly their kinsmen. It was an obligation they owed to their community or native-villages. Most of the maistrys in the mill were Pillais. They had the privilege of bringing their kinsmen and castemen into the mills.

Among the initial recruits of workers, a majority were Naidus who had come to mill B under the inspiration of S.R. Varadarajulu Naidu, a popular union leader in those days. They brought in groups of their people and so were a formidable majority for a time. But the Pillais had entered the higher sphere as maistrys. In course of time, the Mukkulathors succeeded in superseding the Naidus as the majority community among the workers.

The maistrys enjoyed a higher status among the workers. After 1965, there was a downward trend in their status and authority as the jobber system was given up. After that, union leaders became prominent among workers. Their involvement in labour recruitment is notable now. The office staff of the mill are also considerably involved in this.

In the beginning, the management of the mill preferred to recruit persons introduced by their workers. It was believed that the workers introduced by them would not be trouble-mongers. The employees were thus given the privilege to introduce persons in whom they were interested.

In the year 1980, the "varisu" system was introduced in the mill. This system forms one of the recruitment practices in India. The word "varisu" means in Tamil "heir" or "descendent". According to this system, a son of a worker would be provided employment in the mill on his retirement.

This system is, in one way or another, anti-modern and ascriptive. It blocks the chances of skilled and efficient persons who are in search of mill work. Nevertheless, it is more or less a direct check which prevents the corruption of union leaders in labour recruitment. It is also a useful measure to enforce discipline among workers and facilitate labour-management relations.

Within a period of five years, the workes recruited on the basis of the system were twenty. But the system was given up by the management at the end of 1985. The main reason was that there were complaints against a few workers who misused this system. For instance, a worker after his retirement introduced a person as his son. After a few days, it was found that the person not his son. What actually had happened was that the worker had taken Rs. 10,000 from the person for his favour. This resulted in the dismissal of the new recruit. There were two more similar complaints. Consequently, the management has dropped this system.

A similar system is followed even now in the Coimbatore mills studied by Uma Ramaswamy. She points out that though this system is in practice, there are a series of complaints that its implementation leaves much to be desired. The mill jobs are favourably distributed by mill owners, managers and trade union leaders for consideration. Even to get jobs through the "varisu" system, workers must have proper contacts with the management, or at least with the union leaders. Some of the union leaders are not interested in workers' sons being given preference. They often introduce their own candidates.[19]

19. Uma Ramaswamy, *Work, Union and Community* (Delhi: Oxford University Press, 1983), pp. 18-19.

On the other hand, this system has never prevailed in mill A. It was established only a couple of decades back. It comes under the co-operative sector, and it can recruit workers only through the Employment Exchanges of the Government.

In the initial period of mill A, the Chairman of the mill was the administrative authority. There was no compulsion in those days that recruitments should be made through Employment Exchanges. The first Chairman of the mill was a Pillai. He was in the mill from 1964 to 1967. During his period, he recruited a considerable number of his castemen as workers. Still, he was also considerate to workers from other castes.

The second Chairman (1968 to 1970) also belonged to the Pillai caste. It is reported that he was very particular in recruiting his castemen as workers. During his period, a popular Kallar man who was a Legislator belonging to the DMK party elected from Melur constituency, was given the privilege to recommend his candidates for the mill jobs. He introduced a few of his castemen as workers.

The third Chairman who was a notable politician from the DMK party belonged to the Kallar division of the Mukkulathors. He was in the mill from 1970 to 1974. During his tenure, he also recruited his castemen in large numbers. A Naidu politician of the same political party introduced a few of his castemen with the help of the Chairman.

The successive Chairmen and the local politicians thus introduced their castemen in the mill over a period of a decade. The recruitment of workers attained almost a saturation point within this period. In 1974, the State Government implemented a general rule that all recruitments must be made through the Employment Exchanges. The scheduled castes and the backward classes should be given employment based on the reservation policy. From then on appointments have been made through the Employment Exchanges. Consequently, a considerable number of scheduled castes—mostly Paraiyars and a few Pallars—were recruited.

The Managing Board of the mill was dissolved in the year 1975. Since 1975, the mill came under the control of a Managing Director who belonged to IAS Cadre.

It is evident thus that the recruitment of workers in the initial period of mill A was mostly on caste lines. This was the reason why the population of the Kallars (17.9 per cent) in the mill is almost balanced by the population of the Pillais (17.03 per cent). However, the population of Harijans (20.52 per cent) is more sizeable than that of other castemen. This can be explained in three ways. (i) A former minister in the Congress Cabinet in Tamil Nadu was mainly responsible for bringing the mill to this area as he was a native of this area. Since he was a Harijan, he introduced a considerable number of his castemen as workers. (ii) In the recruitments after 1975, the Harijans were given preference, in obedience to the government regulation mentioned above. (iii) In 1978, 237 Sri Lanka Repatriates were recruited as workers under the expansion scheme. As already discussed in fourth chapter, a majority (51.26 per cent) of them belong to the Harijan community.

Caste consideration was also evident in the appointment of staff in the two mills. As regards mill B, in the initial perriod, the Managing Director belonging to the Nagarathar community appointed a Sourashtra as secretary of the mill as he was an expert in cotton and yarn business. He impressed the Managing Director by his ability to run the mill on a good profit. He was given therefore the power to formulate plans for the development of the mill. He filled 70 per cent of the staff positions with his castemen. The key posts in the office were mostly occupied by the Sourashtras. The secretary might have appointed his castemen with the expectation that they would oblige him and also co-operate with him in all his administrative work. The Sourashtras have also earned a reputation as a sincere and hard working group. As the Managing Director trusted the secretary, he never opposed the appointments made by him. The secretary was mainly responsible for the rapid development of the mill and also for the establishment of sixteen sister mills in different places of Tamil Nadu.

A few Nagarathars were also appointed as staff of the mill. They constituted about twenty per cent of the office staff. A few of them were also in key positions. The other ten per cent comprised of men from the Pillai, Brahmin and Agamudaiyar communities.

Though the Nagarathars were only the second largest caste group amon the office staff, they enjoyed certain special privileges. The management gave them special treatment. Once it passed a resolution forbidding the staff from engaging themselves in other remunerative pursuits. This was mainly to check those who were less attentive to their office work due to their involvement in other business. This became a serious problem mainly to the Nagarathars. Most of them were engaged in different trades. They made a representation to the management. At last the resolution was withdrawn for their sake. This is a clear indication of the management's lenience and sympathy to their castemen.

In 1958, the secretary of the mill resigned his post and started a new spinning mill in the outskirts of the southern part of Madurai City. More or less in the same period, a few Sourashtra officials in mill B also resigned and joined the newly established mill out of caste loyalty. Nevertheless, the Sourashtra staff in mill B constituted a majority till 1980.

After the demise of the Managing Director of mill B in 1974, his sons were in charge of the mill for a couple of years. But they were unable to run the mill successfully. Large sums were borrowed from the Central Bank of India for the development of the mill. Since the Bank had a major share in the mill, it took over the management in 1979. It appointed one of its officials as an Executive Director. He was a Mudaliar. During his time, he moderately reshuffled the management staff. He appointed two of his castemen as officers. He was considerate in dealing with the problems of unions. He was in the mill from 1979 to 1982. After his resignation in the year 1982, a Management Committee was formed tentatively to look after the administrative work.

Meanwhile, the Dalmia group purchased a major part of the shares of the mill and took it over in 1982. They thoroughly reshuffled the top management and appointed their kinsmen as officers and managers. They created a few fresh posts mainly to accommodate their kinsmen. They gave their kinsmen key posts in the administrative office. This resulted in the resignation of a few senior officials from other castes.

In this context, it is relevant to refer to the findings of Devadas Pillai. In private sectors, he notes, it is common to create fresh posts to accommodate the relatives of employees.

He observes:

> ...if a top man in a concern wants to get you in, he will get you in—and do not ask how he did it. A large number of organisations that I have come across have no tradition to open recruitment, with the result that even those who are inside an organisation would not know that a few posts have been created, until it is filled.[20]

As far as the office staff of mill A is concerned, it is found that the first and third Chairman appointed one clerk each from their respective castes. But the second Chairman was responsible for the appointment of three of his castemen in the same category. A local politician influenced the management in the appointment of six of his castemen as clerks. One of the Managing Director appointed one of his castemen as a clerk. Altogether twelve clerks (20 per cent) were appointed on caste considerations. They were all appointed before the system of employment through the Employment Exchange came into vogue. The subsequent appointments of staff were on the basis of promotion by seniority and competitive examination and through advertisements in newspapers.

It is clear that caste consideration is a predominant factor not only in the recruitment of workers but also in the appointment of office staff in the two mills.

Nevertheless it is no wonder that caste consideration is

20. S. Devadas Pillai, *Men and Machines* (Bombay: Popular Prakashan, 1968), p. 139.

pronounced in the recruitment of employees in the mills. The caste system still influences the behaviour of Caste-Hindus. It is, therefore, considered to be an usual practice of the people to help their castemen in either employment or other respects. This practice is again evident from the following Table.

Table 13

Respondents by the Nature of Assistance for securing their Jobs

Nature of assistance	*Mill A*	*Mill B*	*Total*
Help of others	61 (62.24)	114 (75.00)	175 (70.00)
Own effort	12 (12.25)	13 (8.55)	25 (10.00)
By other means*	25 (25.51)	25 (16 45)	50 (20.00)
Total	98 (100.00)	152 (100.00)	250 (100.00)

*The other means are "varisu" system and provision by Government.

$x^2=4.644$ df=2 $P>0.05$

A high majority of the respondents (62.24 per cent in mill A and 75 per cent in mill B) have entered service by securing the help of workers of the mill and others. Of the total respondents (98) in mill A, the Mukkulathors and the Pillais constitute nearly one-third each and the rest of them are from other castes. In mill B, of the total respondents (152), the Mukkulathors, the Pillais and the Naidus constitute about one-fourth of the workforce each and the rest of them are from other castes. The reason for this is explained in the previous section. In mill A, 25 (25.51 per cent) respondents who are Sri Lanka Repatriates were recruited as workers under the expansion scheme. This was done as per the direction of the Government. In mill B, 25 (16.45 per cent) respondents got their jobs on the basis of the "varisu" system. Both these categories of respondents had found no difficulty in securing their jobs in the mills.

In mill A, of 61, 51 (83.61 per cent) respondents were helped by the mill employers and employees in their employment, and 98 (85.96 per cent) out of 114 respondents in mill B, belonged to the same category. In the two mills, the percentage of respondents (16.39 per cent in mill A and 14 04 per cent in mill B) helped by outsiders is more or less equal. On the whole a majority of the respondents (52.04 per cent in mill A and 64.47 per cent in mill B) have been helped by the mill employers and employees in their employment. Relatively a low percentage of respondents (12.25 per cent in mill A, and 8.55 per cent in mill B) have secured their jobs by their own efforts, that is, through the Employment Exchange and by responding to advertisements in newspapers. It is noted that most of the staff in the sample (three out of six from mill A and eight out of eleven from mill B) have secured their jobs with the help of others.

It is evident from Table 14 that in mill A, the percentage of respondents (42.86) introduced by their castemen is more or less similar as the percentage of the same category (46.71) in mill B. In the initial period of mill B, the workers especially from the Naidu, Pillai and Mukkulathor castes, introduced their castemen in large numbers. This was, at that time, possible for them as there was less demand for mill jobs. Similarly, in mill A, a large number of respondents were introduced by their castemen. The three successive Chairmen (two were Pillais and one a Kallar) of the mill introduced a considereble number of their castemen as workers. The percentage of the respondents introduced by other castemen in mill B is fairly higher than that of those in mill A.

In mill B, 39 (25.66 per cent) respondents were introduced by the staff from other castes. These helpful staff were mostly the Sourashtras and the Nagarathars. Chapter three explains why these communities were not much interested in mill jobs. Since they were reluctant to take mill jobs, the

Table 14

Respondents by their Mode of Appointment

Nature of Assistance	*Employer*		*Employee*		*Outsiders*		*Respondent himself*		*Other Source*		*Total*	
	A	*B*	*A*	*B*	*A*	*B*	*A*	*B*	*A*	*B*	*A*	*B*
Castemen	17	2	18	57	7	12	—	—	—	—	42 (42.86)	71 (46.71)
Men from other caste	8	—	8	39	3	4	—	—	—	—	19 (19.39)	43 (28.29)
Provision by Government	—	—	—	—	—	—	—	—	25	—	25 (25.51)	—

Varisu system	—	—	—	—	—	—	—	—	—	25	—	25 (16.45)
Own effort	—	—	—	—	—	—	12	13	—	—	12 (12.24)	13 (8.55)
Total	25 (25.51)	2 (1.32)	26 (26.53)	96 (63.16)	10 (10.20)	16 (10.52)	12 (12.25)	13 (8.55)	25 (25.51)	25 (16 45)	98 (100.00)	152 (100.00)

Note: A and B refer to mill A and mill B respectively.

staff of their caste in the mill helped other castemen who approached them for help. All the three staff out of six in mill A and five out of eleven in mill B were introduced by their castemen who were employers as well as employees.

This is supported by the findings of Sheth. He indicates that when vacancies arose or additional jobs were created, the employees already working in the factory came to know about it. Each one of them usually had relatives, castemen, friends or neighbours who were either jobless or looking for factory jobs as better alternatives to their present jobs. Their names were suggested to the workshop superintendent who was in charge of recruitment of workers. In fact the management wanted to recruit such persons. From their point of view, appointing a unknown person would create problems because he might misbehave in any circumstances, whereas appointing a person by considering the recommendation of anyone in the factory was safer. Moreover, the management expected that a person who recommended another person tacitly acknowledged his moral responsibility for the good conduct of the latter and would restrain him from negligence in work, misbehaviour, or trade union activities. So the prescribed form of application which every worker had to fill in at the time of recruitment included a question: Through whom has he (the applicant) come (for the job)?[21]

Similar are the conclusions of many researchers in this field. Devadas Pillai explains that an entrepreneur prefers to have his kinsmen, castemen and villagers for two reasons: he would gain their loyalty, and he can trust them more than others as he would know their background. In large establishments, the departmental heads are given the liberty to bring their "own" people. This is, in a way, beneficial to the employer because the person who brings in new recruits is tacitly held responsible for their conduct and efficiency.[22]

Ramachandra Raj, in his study, finds that a sizeable section of the workers in coir, cashew and plantation

21. N.R. Sheth, *The Social Framework of an Indian Factory* (Bombay: Oxford University Press, 1968), pp. 76-77.
22. Devadas Pillai, *Men and Machines*, p. 57.

industries is recruited from the same caste or sect to which the management belong. However, persons from other castes or sects are also selected for various jobs. When disputes arise between managements and labour, the former usually appeal for support to the caste or sectarian feelings of those among the labour who belong to their own caste or sec.[23]

Baud's study discloses that the recruitment in Coimbatore mills was based mainly on recommendations. The majority (60 per cent) of the women were recommended to the factory manager on the basis of caste affiliation, or being neighbours. A number of women were recruited because they had relatives already working in the mills.[24]

In addition to this it is relevant to compare the ways of recruitment of employees discussed in certain research studies with the trends of recruitment described in the present study. Lambert reports in his study of factories in Pune that more than eighty per cent of workers in the sample factories felt that influence counted most significantly in the matter of appointments. Only about ten per cent of the workers counter this.[25]

In Holmstorms's study, 44 per cent of the respondents reported that they secured jobs only by responding to newspaper advertisements. However, 32 per cent acknowledged that they used influence. But the workers and the management say that at the time of recruitment, only merit is taken into consideration even if anyone gets an interview by influence. Holmstorm points out that "merit" is an ambiguous term. Nevertheless, managements prefer appointing persons whose relatives or friends would vouch for their conduct. All firms give preference to the relatives of

23. G. Ramachandra Raj, *In the Context of Conflicts in the Larger System : A Study of Industrial Conflict in Kerala* (New Delhi : A Research Projects financed by Indian Council of Social Science Research, 1976), p. 60.

24. I.S.A. Baud, *Women's Labour in Indian Textile Industry : The Influence of Technology and Organisation on the Gender Division of Labour*, International Relations and Industrial Structures, Report No. 23 (Tilburg : Tilburg University Press. 1963), p. 69.

25. Lambert, *Workers, Factories and Social Change*, p. 76.

their employees. Some of them try to introduce a "quota" system. His caste studies show that many workers get their jobs through influential persons such as politicians and officials.[26]

Ramaswamy and Uma Ramaswamy find that factories generally advertise vacancies through newspapers and mass media. However, they point out that the personal network of caste, kinship and friendship is still the major means of spreading information with regard to vacancy position in factories. They also indicate that recruitment at the labour level takes place through influence. Prospective recruits bring pressure to bear on managerial personnel, trade union leaders, local influentials, community elders and those already employed in the concern, in order to be considered for employment. They see that jobs are scarce but aspirants many.[27]

Presently the recruitment patterns in mill A and mill B are discussed as follows:

Recruitment in Mill A

The Managing Director of this Co-operative Mill writes to the nearest Employment Exchange about the mill's labour needs. When he gets a list from the Exchange of prospective workers, he makes his selection after a formal interview. He has to set apart a certain percentage of the existing vacancies for scheduled castes and backward classes. Formally, the selection is made by a committee headed by the Chairman.

In the first year of the mill (1965-1966), the recruitment of workers was done through the Employment Exchange. But from 1967 to 1974, direct recruitment by the Chairman was in practice as the mill came under the management of a Board of Directors nominated by the Government. Since 1975, the recruitment is mainly through the Employment Exchange.

26. Mark Holmstrom, *South Indian Factory Workers: Their Life and their World* (Bombay : Allied, 1978), pp. 42-44 and 48.
27. E.A. Ramaswamy and Uma Ramaswamy, *Industry and Labour: An Introduction* (Delhi : Oxford University Press, 1981), p. 9.

Recruitment in Mill B

Union leaders play an important role in the recruitment of workers in mill B. The leaders of the three powerful unions in mill B—the Indian National Trade Union Congress (INTUC), the Panchalai Thozhilalar Munnetra Sangam (PTMS), and the Hindu Mazdoor Sabha (HMS)—bargain with the management and obtain a quota of seats in order to introduce their men whenever vacancies arise. Of the 141 respondents in the mill, 72(51.06 per cent) respondents report that these union leaders can influence the management in the matter of recruitment. The reason is that the management has recognized these three unions.

These union leaders are invited by the management to participate in important discussions pertaining to the problems of the workers. The management also listens to the demands of these leaders and agrees to fulfil them if they are within their limits. These union leaders thus enjoy certain privileges.

At the time of recruitment, many workers seek the help of their union leaders to introduce their men as workers. The leaders would consider those who agree to pay the money demanded by them. Normally, they get between Rs. 5,000 and Rs. 10,000 for one appointment. But they help their kinsmen in this matter without expecting anything from them. Even if a leader feels genuine interest in a candidate recommended by his union worker, he expects money.

In the past decade or so, mostly recruitment of workers has been made on this cash basis. In other words, irrespective of caste loyalties, entry in the mill has been restricted to those who could pay money surreptitiously to the concerned union leaders. This is an interesting development in which the cash factor he also come to play an important role in the case of recruitment. Though the investigator was not able to get authentic data on this, he could gather enough evidence from a few detailed interviews he had with the respondents—both workers and staff in mill B.

Thus caste consideration in the case of abour recruitment has become ineffective as against its influence on a same issue in past decades. In a similar way, class factor has nothing to do with the recruitment. In other words, the activities of the union leaders in this regard do not represent their class behaviour. Instead of selling the seats to those who can afford to pay the prescribed money, the leaders are expected to consider genuine persons recommended by their union members, for labour position. If they do so, it would clearly show their class behaviour. It is important to mention that the investigator never came across such cases during the field work in mill B.

The appointment procedure of the office staff in both the mills differs from the mode of recruitment of workers. All the seventeen staff (sample) of the mills (six in mill A and eleven in mill B) say that they responded to advertisements in the newspapers. However, they report that influence is an essential factor in the appointment of the staff.

Promotions in they Mills

Here promotion mainly refers to the promotion of workers to maistry level and of clerical staff to the next higher level. It is found that the promotion of workers and staff is decided on the basis of seniority as well as influence. In mill A (a co-operative one), the promotion of employees is mostly decided on the basis of seniority and merit. But in mill B (which is under the private sector), the promotion is not strictly decided on the basis of seniority. It mainly depends on the interest of the management in those who are in the promotion list.

In mill B, the promotion of a worker to the maistry position is partly decided on the basis of the influence of union leaders. Nearly one third of the maistrys in mill B came to this position by bribing their union leaders. A few respondents (five) report that they would have become maistrys if they had bribed their union leaders. On the other hand, caste affinity is also partly responsible in this type of promotion. Maistrys are more considerate to their own castemen who have cordial relationship with them in the matter of promotion. Sometimes, they expect money even from workers of their own caste for this favour. In response, workers attend to the personal work of the maistrys. The maistrys specially train them to pick up the skill required to become maistry. For instance, at the time of retirement, a maistry would strongly recommend a worker of his caste who has undergone such training. There are four workers among the respondents who became maistrys mainly due to recommendation.

On the other hand, the promotion in the mill A is by seniority because it is a co-operative spinning mill. However, union leaders recommend their castemen for promotions. For instance, the appointment of an attender in the time-office was highly influenced by a union leader. One respodent who was cheated in this matter describes his experience thus:

> I passed the pre-university course and had more than three years' experience as a worker. The mill management wanted to appoint a qualified worker as an attender in the time-office. I approached my union leader to seek his help. He promised to recommend me for the post as he knew that I was a sincere and active member of the union. But, at the time of appointment, another worker who belonged to his caste but less qualified than me sought his help. The leader changed his mind and strongly recommended him to the Managing Director. Though he did not have the required qualification (a pass in the SSLC examination), he was selected. If he had recommended me, I would have been selected. I am sorry to say that the leader broke his promise simply to favour his castemen. After that I withdrew from that union and joined another union.

This is a clear indication of the way a union leader allows his caste loyalty to suppress his union loyalty.

It is reported that a junior clerical staff in factory is promoted to the post of a Head Timekeeper by the influence of his casteman who is a top official in the factory. A senior clerk who lost this promotion reports:

I am the seniormost among the factory staff. But the top official in the factory did not like my promotion to the post of Head Timekeeper. One of his castemen who is junior to me was assigned to assist his work. He was in the office of the official for a few months. This arrangement was made by the official himself to promote his casteman. Accordingly he recommended him to the then Managing Director for the post of Head Timekeeper. As a result, the junior clerk is promoted to that post.

However, this type of anomaly can be checked by the authorities in the co-operative sector at least in course of time. This is what happened in the mill at the time of data collection. The present Managing Director who is said to be a stickler to the rules stipulated by the Government, came to know of this anomaly and other problems of the staff. He moderately reshuffled the staff both in the main office and in the factory. Due to this, the clerk who was promoted to position of the Head Timekeeper was transferred to the main office as clerk. The senior clerk who lost the promotion chance was posted as Head Timekeeper. Similarly, a senior attender in the factory belonging to the Harijan community was denied promotion for a long time because his immediate head was not favourably disposed to him. He was often humiliated by his head with a view to sending him out of his department. But now the attender is promoted as an assistant in the main office.

In this regard, the investigator interviewed the respondents and obtained information pertaining to the promotion procedures, individually from their point of view. The data so obtained are described hereunder.

A majority of the respondents (63.27 per cent) in mill A say that promotion is through seniority, whereas a fairly high percentage of respondents (33.45 per cent) in mill B state that promotion is through the influence of a few employees in the same mill. These influential employees include union leaders and maistrys. In mill A, promotion through the influence of employees of the same caste is twice as much as promotion through the influence of employees of other castes. But in mill B, the percentage of these two categories is more or less equal. It is also seen that the number of those who acknoledged that they secured their promotion through bribing is four times higher than the number of those in the same category in mill A. All the six staff in mill A and only four staff in mill B say that the promotion is by seniority.

Table 15

Respondents by their Views on Promotion

Factors for promotion	*Mill A*	*Mill B*	*Total*
Seniority	62 (63.27)	29 (19.08)	91 (36.40)
Influence of other employers and employees	23 (23.47)	51 (33.55)	74 (29.60)
Bribing the employees	5 (5.10)	31 (20.40)	36 (14.40)
No idea	8 (8.16)	41 (26.97)	49 (19.60)
Total	98 (100.00)	152 (100.00)	250 (100.00)

$x^2=54.439$ df=3 $P<0.001$

As found in the recruitment of employees in the mills, the class factor does not influence their promotion too. The presence of class behaviour of the workers and staff would be identified by their protest against the influence of management persons in the promotion of employees. However, the investigator did not come across such protest of employees against management. Therefore this shows that the workers united by their union and the employees by their association, are not aware of their class action to prevent any influence of caste on promotion and other aspects.

It is expected that, in a privately owned industry, the class awareness would emerge when the management tries to sustain its interest by prevailing over the worker-class. On the contrary, this awareness among the workers in the mill B is curtailed by factors like management's policy of divide and rule in the case of unions, multi-unionism and corruptive nature of union leaders.

On the other hand, in any co-operative or public sector undertaking, it is the people's will in principle that ultimately governs. The top echelons of this sector are occupied by the Government's nominees. They function on democratic methods and the governance of this sector is on the basis of clearly stipulated rules and regulations. It is therefore assumed that the class awareness among the employees in the sector may not emerge for class action against the management. This is, in one way or another, true in the case of mill A.

There is strong evidence to show that the managements in the mill come to a fair understanding with the union leaders in their promotion or emloyment of some workers so that the union leaders may have their own choice in these respects. This is done with a view to appease the union leaders so that they may not indulge in the instigation of strikes even in the context of legitimate demands. This procedure under minesthe workers' faith or trust in their union leaders. This attitude of the managements prevents the workers from coming together as aclass. In other words, unionism is not here and now the road to the union of the workers. In this manner the higher hegemony is sustained and strengthened with the help of the very tools, namely the union leaders, which are supposed to develop class-consciousness among the workers. This has been discussed elaborately in the VI Chapter.

5

Interacting Situations of Employees

The advent of modern technology with its characteristic industrial organisations leads to the general expectation that the nature of employment will no longer be determined by ascribed status or hereditary distinctions like caste. Also there is another expectation like the forms of interaction among the workers transcending the caste, religion or other cultural barriers. It would be interesting to see how far the data collected in this study either confirm or contradict these general expectations.

The employees of an industry have to interact with one another in either formal or informal or in both situations for various reasons irrespective of their age, caste and religion. The interacting situation among the employees is mostly concerned with their activities relating to production in the industry. It is normally limited due to the concentration on work on the shopfloor. This interaction, connected with the discharge of their official duty, is formal. But all their interaction is not limited to their workspot, nor is it all formal. Any interaction among them beyond the official purview is informal.

In this chapter, an attempt is made to study the group evel interaction of the respondents that is, their nature of linteraction with other employees both in formal and informal situations. Further, an attempt is made to study the individual level interaction of the repondents, that is, their nature of interaction with their friends. In other words, this chapter tries to find the relative involvement of caste or class relations in these interacting situations.

Group Level Interaction

There are, in each of the mills, twelve departments in the production line. All the departments are accommodated in one big block of buildings. Every department, however, is compartmentalised and self-contained, though it is within easy access to all the other departments. Thus picking up casual acquaintances in other departments, or even establishing close ties of friendship with men of the other departments, is not difficult.

This investigation is the most superficial level of this study. It merely goes to show that the respondents who come from various castes, are capable of making acquaintance with employees from all the departments of the mill.

The respondents were asked to mention their level of interaction with other employees in the corresponding occupational category. Their interaction is classified into three levels : "wider", that is, interaction with many employees in all departments; "moderate", that is, interaction with all employees in their departments but with limited employees in other departments and "limited", that is, interaction with only selected employees in some departments. The respondents are distributed into these three levels of interaction according to their castes as shown in Table 16.

The Table shows that in both the mills a majority of the respondents have a moderate capacity to pick up casual acquaintance with other employees. There is, therefore, no significant relationship between caste or location of the mills and the interaction of the respondents. The Mukkulothors (48 per cent) in mill A and the Pillais (41.38 per cent) and Harijans (40 per cent) in mill B interact widely with men from other departments. But these data do not take us deeper into the question it does not show whether this interaction amounts

Table 16

Respondents by their Caste and their Interaction with other Employees

Caste	*Interaction of the respondents with other employees*						*Total*	
	Wider		*Moderate*		*Limited*			
	Mill A	*Mill B*	*Mill A*	*Mill B*	*Mill A*	*Mill B*	*Mill A*	*Mill B*
1	*2*	*3*	*4*	*5*	*6*	*7*	*8*	*9*
Mukkulathor	12 (48.00)	24 (41.38)	10 (40.00)	28 (48.28)	3 (12.00)	6 (10.34)	25 (100.00)	58 (100.00)
Pillai	5 (29.41)	8 (38.10)	9 (52.94)	10 (47.62)	3 (17.65)	4 (14.28)	17 (100.00)	21 (100.00)
Naidu	1 (14.29)	7 (26.92)	4 (57.14)	15 (57.69)	2 (28.57)	4 (15 39)	7 (100.00)	26 100.00)

(*Contd.*)

1	*2*	*3*	*4*	*5*	*6*	*7*	*8*	*9*
Scheduled Caste	7 (36.84)	4 (40.00)	8 (42.11)	4 (40.00)	4 (21.05)	2 (20.00)	19 (100.00)	10 (100.00)
Other castes	13 (43.33)	13 (35.13)	15 (50.00)	17 (45.95)	2 (6.67)	7 (18.92)	30 (100.00)	37 (100.00)
Total	38 (38.78)	56 (36.84)	46 (46.94)	74 (48 69)	14 (14.28)	22 (14.37)	98 (100.00)	152 (100.00)

Mill A (Caste-wise) : $x^2=5.946$ df=8 P>0.05

Mill B (Caste-with) : $x^2=3.151$ df=8 P>0.05

Mill A and Mill B (location-wise) : $x^2=0.083$ df=2 P>0.05.

to the establishment of interaction that disregards caste affinities. A more complete picture should be able to suggest what factors are responsible for the nature and composition of the employees' level of interaction. The next stage of our study takes up that issue.

The data presented in Table 16 may be explained in this manner. The Mukkulathors who constitute the majority in mill A come to work daily in groups from the surrounding villages by bicycles or buses. So the non-work situation promotes constant interaction among them. They are widely represented in all the departments of the mill. This may be the reason why they interact with many workers in all the departments. Workers from other castes, such as the Pillais and Naidus, are mostly migrants; they do not live in close proximity to the mill. Their residences are scattered in and around Melur town. They are, therefore, not able to move in groups to their workspot. Since their interaction with others in non-work situation is restricted, they interact moderately with other workers on the shopfloor.

The Harijan workers and staff of mill A still live in their colonies (*Parai cheri*) secluded from the main stream of the village community. Presumably they have not yet outgrown their caste inhibitions. This may be the reason why their interaction with others in the mill is also moderate. But the Harijan workers of mill B live amidst the Caste-Hindus in the residential areas adjacent to the mill. This might have removed their inhibitions and made them free in their interaction with the Caste-Hindu workers. So they interact with many workers from other departments.

With regard to staff, most of them (four in mill A and seven in mill B) interact moderately with other staff. The probing of the factors responsible for the limited interaction of the respondents leads up to interesting conclusions.

In both the mills, it turns out, they are afraid of one community—the Mukkulathors. The details and relevance of the impact of this community on the inter-caste atmosphere in the two mills is discussed in due course.

It is interesting to note that the respondents whose interaction is limited because of the riotous behaviour of the

Table 17

Respondents by Reasons for their Limited Interaction

Reasons	*Respondents* Mill A	Mill B	*Total*
Devoted to work and not concerned with others' affairs	5	10	15
Riotous behaviour of the Mukkulathors	8	10	18
Reserved by nature	1	2	3
Total	14	22	36

Mukkulathors are more in number than those who gave reasons such as devotion to work and being reserved by nature. The former say that they often avoid interacting with the Mukkulathors who constitute the majority in both the mills. They also indicate that if any employee from other castes opposes either a Kallar or a Maravar, he will be put into trouble or even killed in retaliation.

It is seen that in mill B there is no inter-caste rivalry strong enough to lead to fights. But in mill A, it can be seen that the Mukkulathors' capacity for wider interaction is not an indication of openness or friendliness. On the other hand, it indicates their tendency to stick to their own people for acquaintance. Mill A is dominated by the Mukkulathors and workers from that caste are found in large numbers in all the departments. In mill B also, numerically they are the dominant group. Their caste loyalties lead them to wider interaction with their counterparts in the other departments. This solidarity is evidently an inhabiting influence on the workers from other castes.

In mill A, the respondents who had differences with the Kallar and the Maravar workers uniformly say that they are rough in their approach and become violent when they have differences with others. They also indicate that the Kallars and the Maravars presume that they are privileged workers. This is according to them, mainly because of their numerical strength not only in the mill but also in the surrounding areas. They point out that usually workers of other castes move cautiously with the Kallars and the Maravars because of their violent nature and riotous behaviour at the time of conflicts. They hold the view that the Kallars resort to violence even over simple matters, especially when the other party belongs to some other caste. More or less the same view is held by other respondents (five Pillais, two Naidus and one each from the Sourashtra, Reddiyar and Nadar castes) who have not come in conflict with either the Kallars or the Maravars.

This view is further corroborated by the Assistant Factory Manager (who is a Nadar) with whom the investigator had an informal discussion. He says that he has gained rich experience in dealing with workers from different castes in the mill. He describes the Kallars thus:

> The Kallars are emotional in nature. They behave mostly in a rough manner. Therefore, I adopt my own method to deal with them. If a Kallar worker approaches me for any problem, I pretend to be very strict and also deal with him very firmly. Instead of this, if I deal with him in a casual way, he will talk too much and his very approach will be quarrelsome.

In mill A, there was tension between the local Mukkulathor workers and workers who come from the Tamil refugee families from Sri Lanka and the migrant families of Naidus and Pillais. Especially the refugees and the Naidus feel that they are near aliens in this place. In mill B, there is no such refugee population. But a big number of the Naidus from Srivilliputhur joined the mill some thirty years back. They constitute the migrant population of this mill. They are invariably Vaishnavites, and they have named the area of their settlements after the Vaishnavite saint-poetess Andal. This is the Andalpuram area adjacent to the mill. Nearly 85 per cent of the present population of this area are the Naidus working in the mill. Nearby lies the residential area called

Sundararajapuram, the majority of whose inhabitants are workers of the mill belonging to the Mukkulathor caste. The residential area called Alagaradi, near the Madura Coats, is predominantly an area of the Pillais who work in mill B and the Madura Coats. In the decades of their established life in Madurai, the migrant Naidus of mill B have shed their feeling of difference and any sense of inferiority as new-comers to the place. But in mill A, the migrant workers from Ceylon and from the Pillai and the Naidu castes keep away as far as possible from conflicts with the Mukkulathors due to a feeling of insecurity.

However, it can be seen that caste discrimination and ill-treatment of the lower castes are not much in evidence. The industrial atmosphere seems to have blunted the edge of such discrimination. In her compilation of the findings of studies on the textile workers of Kanpur, Chitra Joshi presents a situation where discrimination is still an inescapable fact of life. She finds that the workers of the higher caste were particular that their lunch packets should not be polluted by the touch of any *chamar* ("untouchable" caste) or Muslim worker. In case any one of them touched the packets, they would consider it their right to be paid in cash for their food in exchange for the "defiled" packets. Further she finds that dry *chabena* was the food for most of the Brahmins as they would not eat any cooked food while they were in contact with "unclean" castes. She points out that the dining shed in a mill was used only by a few workers, because the large number of Brahmin workers had their lunch outside it.[1]

But the observation that the industrial atmosphere counters the traditional caste-relations is reinforced by Kuthiala's remarks on the inter-caste relationship among the industrial workers in two privately-owned factories in North India.[2] It is this observation that gets confirmed in the present study. A majority of the Caste-Hindu respondents (86.08 per cent in mill A and 89.44 per cent in mill B) say that they move with the Harijans without any reservation. Nevertheless, some respondents (13.92 per cent in mill A and 10.56 per cent

1. Chitra Joshi, "Kanpur Textile Labour," pp. 1823-1838.
2. Kuthiala, *From Tradition to Modernity*, p. 138.

in mill B) state that they keep to a minimum their interaction with the Harijans. This is, they report, mainly due to the indecent behaviour of the Harijans. But they do not go out of their way to avoid physical contact with the latter.

All the Harijan respondents (19 in mill A and 10 in mill B) in the sample were asked to answer the question with regard to the avoidance behaviour of employees belonging to other castes. All of them say that they are not avoided by others for pollution. They also point out that they move with others without inhibitions and dine with them in the canteens both inside and outside the mills.

Holmstorm's observation confirms this. He says that all the rules about the contact between castes are irrelevant in many situations for most people and in all situations for some people. Almost all the workers eat with Harijans in factory canteens. Most of them say that they have friends from different castes.[3] Thus industries, by and large, lead to circumstances that facilitate relationships and lessen differences and feelings of superiority or inferiority.

The investigator found in these two mills an atmosphere of relative friendliness prevailing at the moment. There were no lasting tensions originating from caste rivalries. Occasionally bickerings snowballed into caste conflicts and temporarily disturbed the atmosphere. But they did not for long continue as caste conflicts.

From the study of contacts to the study of conflicts is a natural development. The preceding first phase of this study, and the present one that deals with conflicts, are both studies of group-level responses. At both these levels, it is found that caste is an influencing force to reckon with. Even conflicts that start at the individual level quickly take on caste overtones, so that it becomes evident that only peripherally caste discrimination has lessened. But even that is not to be under-estimated in its significance.

An overwhelming majority of the respondents in the mills (83.67 per cent in mill A and 88.82 per cent in mill B) indicate that they have affable relationship with those with

3. Holmstrom, *South Indian Factory Workers*, p. 80.

whom they interact. However, there are certain incidents of conflict between the respondents and other employees.

Table 18

Respondents by Inter-caste Conflict in Mill A

Caste of the employees with whom the respondents had conflict	*Caste of the respondents*					
	Pillai	*Naidu*	*Konar*	*Valaiyar*	*Harijan*	*Total*
Kallar	2	2	1	1	2	8
Maravar	2	1	—	—	1	4
Naidu	2	—	—	—	—	2
Total	6	3	1	1	3	14

It is found that in mill A, out of fourteen, eight incidents of conflict were between the Kallar workers on the one hand and the Pillai, Naidu, Konar, Valaiyar and Harijan respondents (workers) on the other; four were between the Maravar workers on the one hand and the Pillai, Naidu and Harijan respondents (workers) on the other; two were between the Naidu and Pillai respondents who are staff in factory. It is also important to note that of the fourteen, eleven incidents of conflict were verbal in nature and the other three among workers culminated in physical assault. Cross checks were also made in order to get a clear perspective on these incidents of conflict.

It appears that inter- and intra-union rivalry is the main cause for these conflicts. But they have their roots in caste rivalry. The conflicts which resulted in physical assault seem to have some relevance in this context.

A Pillai respondent who had a conflict with a Kallar reports that the Kallars have strong caste feelings. For instance, he says, if there is a conflict between a Kallar and a man of another caste, the former readily recalls on his kinsmen and castemen for support. In order to substantiate this view, he recalled an incident.

> In 1980, there was a verbal fight between a Kallar worker and a Velar worker on the shopfloor of the mill. The latter somehow guessed that the Kallar would attack him outside the mill. Therefore, he approached members of his union including me except the Mukkulathors and sought our help for his protection. He also requested us to wait in front of the mill gate. When the shift was over, he came out of the mill. As anticipated by him, the Kallar attacked him. But the Velar's union friends who were near the gate separated them and assaulted the Kallar. Angered by his act, I got wild and beat him severely. The wounded man rushed to the neighbouring town and gave his version of the incident to his kinsmen and castemen. Since it was late in the evening, they were not able to do anything that day. The next morning, the Kallar along with a group of his kinsmen and castemen waited in a place a little away from the mill. When I crossed that place unsuspectingly, I was forcibly dragged into their midst and beaten severely. As I swooned with severe injuries, I was thrown on the road like a dead animal. But neither my kinsmen nor castemen came forward to enquire into this as they feared that the Kallars who constituted a majority in the area would do anything against them if an enquiry took place.

The conflict between a Kallar and a Konar (shepherd caste) was the result of their contest in the DMK-backed union (PTMS) regarding the election to the president's post. In the election, the Kallar candidate was defeated. He could not brook a Konar becoming the President of the union. As a result, he often opposed the views of the President. Besides, he secretly incited men of his caste in the union to go counter to the President. The hostility led to physical assault on the President by a few Kallars. Every one knew that this had happened mainly due to the vengeful attitude of the Kallar.

This was, at that time, the talk of the mill. Many of the workers felt that it was an injustice, but none of them raised his voice against the Kallar. Nor did the Kallar members of the union came forward to correct him with the intention that such incidents should not recur. They did not like a Konar to be the President of their union. The Secretary of the union who was a Pillai did not even discuss this with members of his caste who were more or less numerically equal to the Kallars in the unions as he feared that the Kallars would gang up and do whatever they like. As last the helpless Konar had to pocket the insult as he felt that he could not do anything against the Kallar without tne cooperation of the members of his union.

An attempt was made to get the views of the Kallar and Maravar workers towards those respondents with whom they had quarrelled. They feel that the Pillais and the Naidus have a strong caste feeling and mostly help their castemen. They say that these persons try to dominate the unions such as the PTMS, the ATS and the INTUC. But they do not have any specific views on either the Konar or the Valaiyar with whom they had conflicts.

It is important to mention here that there are only four migrant respondents involved in such conflicts as against twelve non-migrants. The migrants normally feel that they have to be very careful in adjusting themselves with the natives of the area where they live because they are strangers to their customs and activities. Moreover, they are afraid that they would be troubled by the native Kallars of the area in which circumstances they could hardly gain the support of others.

Though there is no evidence to support this, it is relevant here to mention the views of a few migrant respondents with whom the investigator had an informal discussion after the interview was over. Two of them were Harijans, one a Naidu, another a Velar and the last one a Konar. They all say this about the Kallars:

> We are always careful in moving with the Kallars of this area, especially the Kallar workers of the mill, because

they are, by nature, rough in their approach. They quarrel even over petty things and become furious at the time of conflict. Generally, migrants like us should be very careful in this area as we are envied by the Kallars inside as well as outside the mill. If they do not like any migrant worker for any reason, they warn him: "You are an alien to our place; you have come here for your survival; you have to adjust yourself with us; if you do anything against us, you will be liquidated". At the time of cur settlement here, we were afraid of them and as a result we were not able to live a fearless life.

In the mill, the Kallars are the rivals to the Pillais both on the shopfloor and at the office. Each caste tries to dominate over the other one as the two castes are, more or less, numerically equal (172 Kallars and 171 Pillais) in the universe. This has been the trend since the inception of the mill.

Such inter-caste conflicts are noted in mill B too.

Table 19

Respondents by Inter-caste Conflcit in Mill B

Caste of the workers with whom the respondents had conflict	*Caste of the respondents*			*Total*
	Naidu	*Pillai*	*Maravar*	
Kallar	4	3	1	8
Maravar	3	3	—	6
Agamudaiyar	2	2	—	4
Total	9	8	1	18

This table shows that the conflict is between the Mukkulathor workers on the one hand and workers from other castes such as the Naidu and the Pillai on the other. It is found that there has been one conflict between a Kallar and a Maravar. It is also found that only the shopfloor workers are involved in conflicts. However, none of the conflicts has resulted in physical assault. The investigator made cross references to ascertain the facts relating to their conflicts.

All the Pillai and Naidu respondents uniformly state that the Mukkulathors are their rivals. The Mukkulathor workers with whom these respondents conflicted report that the Naidus are their main rivals. They also mention that the Pillais are also their rivals to a certain extent.

The investigator tried to get at the truth of all their reports. He picked up the acquaintance of two senior maistrys—one a Naidu and another a Pillai. They had served the same mill for thirty-five years and so had a sound knowledge of the history of the mill. The investigator interviewed them extensively. The information provided by them corresponds by and large. Besides the investigator interviewed two other senior maistrys—a Maravar and an Agamudaiyar—in order to get corroborative evidence. The information given by them also corresponds with the version of the first pair. In addition, the information provided by a senior Pillai officer with whom the investigator had an informal discussion also confirms their information. The gist of their reports is given below:

> In the early 1930s, S.R. Varadarajulu Naidu was Secretary of the Madras Labour Union. He wanted to establish a union in Madurai with the support of mill workers. After some time, he gained by his popularity the support of the workers from his caste and other castes. As a result, "The Madura Labour Union" was established. He had a large number of supporters from the Madura Mills (the erstwhile name of the Madura Coats) and mill B as these mills recruited a large number of Naidus who, at that time, used to come forward to join the mills.
>
> S.R. Varadarajulu Naidu did not take any step to gain the support of the workers in the Mahalakshmi Mills which had been established in Madurai. There were two reasons for this. Naidu was mainly waging his campaign

against the Madura Coats; and the workers in the Mahalakshmi Mills were predominantly from the Maravar and Kallar divisions of the Mukkulathor. The Mukkulathors of that mill wanted to have a popular leader of their caste to safeguard their interest. The late political leader of the Mukkulathor caste, Pasumpon Muthuramalinga Thevar, visited the mill to learn the condition of the workers of his caste.

Making use of this opportunity, they requested him to solve their problems by organising a union in the mill. He organised "The Mahalakshmi Textile Workers' Union" and he enlisted the support of the Communist members for this union. He became the nominal leader of this union. This was the first rival Madura Labour Union. After sometime, he also visited mill B to form a union. After discussions with the management of the mill, he formed a union there with the support of the workers belonging to his caste. It was Muthuramalinga Thevar's great prestige that gave the mill worker a sense of pride in his job. From this time, the Mukkulathors came forward to join the mills (in large numbers).

The Thevar union in the Mahalakshmi Mill put forward to the management a number of demands including the recognition of the union and the reinstatement of some workers who had been dismissed for complaining against the management. But the management turned down their demand and also dismissed the leaders of the Thevar union from service. Naidu supported the management in this regard. The workers of the Thevar union were angered by the attitude of Naidu. They wanted to end the domination of the Naidu union. The power struggle between the unions manifested itself in big meetings of the rival unions. The followers of the two unions, thus, developed a hostility towards each other.

After sometime, Naidu organised a strike with his supporters in the Mahalakshmi Mills to press certain demands. But the Thever union strongly opposed it. Similarly, another strike organised by the Naidu union in mill B in relation to bonus was opposed by the Thevar union. In the Madura Coats also, the supporters of the two unions opposed each other on several issues. The Pillai workers were also in opposition to the Naidus as they did not like the domination of the Naidus. However, unlike the Thevars, their opposition to the Naidus was not very keen.

One evening, when Naidu was addressing a meeting of his followers near mill B, telling them to oppose the mill owners and the rival union, the supporters of the Thevar union and the Pillais of mill B and the Mahalakshmi Mill disturbed the meeting. This resulted in conflict between the two unions and led to the murder of Pillai by a Naidu.

The rivalry between the supporters of the two unions thus arose out of caste rivalries between the leaders.

Neverthelesss this conflict is also due to the instigation by the management of mill B. This is inferred from the information provided by the four senior maistrys. The management wanted to do away with the domination of Naidu union so that it would not counter the management for the cause of workers. Therefore, when Muthuramalinga Thevar came for a discussion with the management to form a union in mill B, they willingly supported him to do so. Consequently, he formed a union there with the support of his caste workers. The management thought that the newly formed union would be a suitable rival to suppress the domination of Naidu union.

It is an interesting example as how the management keep the workers in a state of conflict by carefully dividing them into groups. This 'divide and rule' policy is followed by industrial management elsewhere to get over the problems arouse out of labour union. This is supported by the analysis of inter and intra-union conflicts in the V chapter. It is clear that the management deliberately divide the workers into rival groups by instigating the powerful union cordial relationship. The management is thus divisive force which carefully prevent the emergence of class consciouness by disintegrating the workers with the help of their union leaders.

After 1947, there was a change in mill workers in Madurai. The Madura Labour Union all but disappeared. It is supposed to be alive now, though it has no place in the union map of mill B. More or less in the same period, the Mahalakshmi Textite Workers' Union was dissolved. The new unions were not caste-oriented; they sought to unite all mill workers in particular, and all workers in general. There are several unions now in each mill and workers join them according to their inclinations.

But even today, the old rivalry between the Mukkulathors and the Naidus live in the minds of the older employees of mill B. It also continues in the minds of the younger generation as a legacy. The rate of increase in the numerical strength of the Mukkulathors in the mill is higher than that of the Naidus in recent years. Since the early 1970s, the Mukkulathors have been the dominant caste in the mill. The Naidus resent the fact that their dominant position in the mill has been taken over by the Mukkulathors. This is one reason for the continued rivalry in the mill between these two castes.

The rivalry between the Pillais and the Mukkulathors in the mill may also be explained in terms of the domination of the Mukkulathors. Like the Naidus, the Pillais also joined the mill in the initial period, but not in large numbers. Till 1970, they occupied the second place in terms of the numerical strength. Most of the maistrys were Pillais and they wielded command over the workers of the mill. After 1970, the Mukkulathors constitute the majority in the mill. Some of them have moved to the position of maistrys and union leaders within a decade, leaving the Pillais behind. This has developed a feeling of rivalry among the Pillais towards the Mukkulathors.

The intra-caste conflict among the employees is noted mostly in mill B. In the mill, six incidents of such conflicts took place a few months before the period of data-collection for this study. Two of them were between the Maravars and four between the Kallars and the Maravars. It is reported that none of the conflicts resulted in physical assault. All these conflicts originated in union elections. They arose out of the question as to who was to contest the union elections. One or two workers of each division of the Mukkulathor caste wanted to compete for the post of President or Secretary.

Such conflicts are not found among the three dtvisions of tbe Mukkulathor caste in mill A. The reason may be that the Kallars are relatively a more aggressive and domineering lot than the other two. As they constitute the majority (about 73 per cent) among the Mukkulathors, their leadership qualities may find easy assertion and prevail over the other two divisions. Thereby there could be no scope for internal conflicts among the Mukkulathors of mill A. But in mill B, the Agamudaiyars constitute the majority (about 57 per cent) among the Mukkulathors. They arc found to be a less aggressive lot with limited leadership ambitions in contrast to the Kallars and the Maravars. Possibly the Kallars and the Maravars in mill B indulge in rivalries for assuming leadership position which leads to intra-caste conflicts.

The respondents in the offices of the mills (two Pillais, a Kallar and a Harijan in mill A and three Sourashtras, two Nagarathars and a Pillai in mill B) approach men of their own caste in the same rank for these purposes.

The investigator observed the interaction among the staff especially during lunch-break. The Sourashtras and Nagarathars in mill B engaged in casual conversation with the colleagues of their own caste to while away the rest time after lunch. Sometimes, they formed small groups within the office to discuss their personal problems. Their interaction was mostly along caste lines during working hours too. One respondent from the staff who is a Pillai comments thus on the interaction of the Sourashtras.

> The Sourashtras mostly move with their castemen. They have limited relationship with men of other castes in the office. For instance, if a Sourashtra from the main

> office comes to the time-office, it is certain that he would meet one of his castemen. After discussing official or non-official matters with him, he does not even look at his other colleagues in the office. Unless the situation warrants, he would not normally meet colleagues of other castes. Generally, the Sourashtras do not share their knowledge of official dealings with junior colleagues from other castes. I think they do not believe their colleagues from other castes. Like them, the Nagarathars mostly restrict their movements to their own castemen. The staff from these two castes have more caste solidarity than the staff from other castes.

The investigator observed in mill A that a few members of the staff belonging to the Pillai caste, after lunch, formed a small group to while away their rest time. A few Naidus did so too. A similar trend was found among the staff from the Mukkulathor caste. But, generally, the staff from various castes move freely with one another. A Harijan who is an attender in the main office explains that the staff from the Pillai, Naidu and Mukkulathor castes have more caste feeling than others.

> I was previously an attender in the factory office. My immediate head was a Pillai. A few Pillai staff joined him during lunch break for discussing their personal problems and other matters concerning the mill. In such a situation, he did not like my presence there. He influenced the then Managing Director of the mill to transfer me to the main office. After sometime I was transferred to the main office as an attender. Like my previous head, a staff from Naidu caste occupying a key position in the factory tried to form a group of his own castemen. Similarly, most of the staff from the Mukkulathor caste form a group for discussing their problems.

Thus, in the two mills, it is not the consciousness of a working class that dominates among the workers. As has already been pointed out, caste loyalties, caste rivalries and a feeling of insecurity in having to be amidst the Mukkulathors drive a wedge between workers belonging to different castes. In some cases, the conflicts surface unmistakably; in other cases, they manifest themselves more subtly and surreptitiously. But the inescapable fact is that the workers are not able to trust themselves and to instil in themselves a feeling of class-consciousness.

Individual Level Interaction

The next phase of this work moves from group level interaction to a deeper, individual level—to establish personal contact for certain purposes among the workers of the two mills. If personal relationship could cut across caste affinities, they would naturally soften down the irritants in group interactions. But group-level interaction and personal-level interaction are inextricably interrelated. Since in the earlier finding (that in group level interaction) caste considerations weigh somewhat significantly, we can take as proved its corollary that in personal level interaction also caste considerations weigh. The following sections elucidate the process by which this proposition was tested.

A list of statements was prepared trying to elicit the respondents' preferences in individual contacts in their workspots. The few minutes between their arrival at the workspot and the actual commencement of the work, the interval for lunch, and the journey from and to homeward are the usual moments of informal interaction. Five situations conducive to personal interaction were identified as selective indicators of caste loyalty in personal interacting situations: casual conversation, seeking help for problems other than monetary need, seeking monetary assistance, discussing vital domestic problems in search of solutions, and sharing personal joys and sorrows. The respondents were asked to specify their first choice of friends for these purposes. They were also asked to exclude their kinsmen from this list because of the reason that both interacting with kinsmen and making friends with them are very common: they have mutual obligation to one another.

The rural-urban background of the respondents has its impact on their choice of friends from among their colleagues for such purpose. This is shown in Table 20.

The Table shows that an average of 73.2 per cent of respondents in mill A have personal contacts with men among their colleagues in the mill for these purposes and in mill B, an average of 89.2 per cent do so. The rest of the respondents in these two mills resort to friends who are outside the mill.

An average of 60.20 per cent of the respondents in mill A prefer friends from their own caste for these purposes; in mill B, this category of respondents constitutes an average of 33.29 per cent of the sample. There is thus a significant relationship between the background of the respondents and their choice of friends. The significant relationship between the two variable is shown in Table 21.

It can be seen that a little variation from this pattern relates to the matter of contacts for monetary help. In both the mills, a fairly high percentage of respondents seek the help of people outside their caste-fold in the mill on financial matters. It is pointed out that some workers practise money-lending as a secondary occupation and a worker in financial need has to go to these colleagues irrespective of their caste. In this case, the relationship between the background of the respondents and their choice of men for seeking monetary assistance is significant but not very high as found in other cases.

It is not surprising that the respondents' choice of friends for these purposes is influenced by caste considerations. A majority of the shopfloor workers of both the mills belong to the Mukkulathor caste. Workers from other castes, such as the Pillais, the Harijans and the Naidus, constitute a fairly high percentage of the population in the mills. They approach workers of their caste for such purposes. In spite of this, there is a significant difference between mill A and mill B with regard to this choice of the respondents. In other words, the

Table 20

Respondents by their first Choice of Friends for Personal Contacts

Reasons for personal contacts	*No. of respondents whose friends are their own castemen*		*No. of respondents whose friends are only from other caste*		*No. of respondents who have no friends within the mill*		*Total*	
	Mill A	*Mill B*	*Mill A*	*Mill B*	*Mill A*	*Mill B*	*Mill A*	*Mill B*
Casual conversation	66 (67.35)	59 (38.82)	17 (17.35)	51 (33.55)	15 (15.30)	42 (27.63)	98 (100.00)	151 (100.00)
Seeking help for problems other than monetary need	63 (64.29)	51 (33.55)	13 (13.27)	27 (17.76)	22 (22.44)	74 (48.69)	98 (100.00)	152 (100.00)
Seeking monetary assistance	53 (54.08)	51 (33.55)	26 (26 53)	42 (27.63)	19 (19.39)	59 (38.82)	98 (100.00)	152 (100.00)
Discussing vital domestic problems in search of solutions	58 (59.18)	41 (26.97)	8 (8.16)	32 (21.05)	32 (32.66)	79 (51.98)	98 (100.00)	152 (100.00)
Sharing personal joys and sorrows	55 (56 12)	51 (33.55)	7 (7.14)	41 (26.97)	36 (36.74)	60 (39.48)	98 (100.00)	152 (100.00)

Table 21

Relationship be'ween the Background of Respondents and their Choice of Friends

Purpose of cantant	*Chi-square*	*Degrees of freedom*	*P*
Casual conversation	19.424	2	P<0.05
Seeking help for problems other than monetary need	23.775	2	P<0.05
Seeking monetary assistance	13.271	2	P<0.05
Discussing vital domestic problems in search of solution	26.806	2	P<0.05
Sharing personal joys and sorrows	19.478	2	P<0.05

respondents' choice of friends is more pronouncedly along caste lines in mill A than in mill B.

This may be explained in terms of the rural-urban background of the respondents. It is understood from the sample that more respondents in mill A (63.27 per cent) than in mill B (46.71 per cent) come from villages. It is possible that knowingly or unknowingly they carry to the mills their custom and practices which are mostly governed by their castes. Hence the difference between the two mills in relation to the respondents' choice of friends among their colleagues.

Like rural-urban background, caste factor also influences the respondents in the matter of preferring friends for those purposes. The aim is to know whether there is significant variation among the respondents from different castes with reference to their preference of friends.

There is a similarity between the Mukkulathors and the Pillais in respect to first choice of friends for those purposes. It is found that more or less a majority of the respondents (an average of 48.91 per cent of the Mukkulathors and 50 per cent of Pillais) prefer friends from their own castes for those purposes. In a similar way, the Naidus and Harijans are more

Table 22

Respondents (Caste-wise) by their first Choice of Friends for Personal Contacts

Reasons for personal contact	*Mukkulathor*			*Pillai*		
	I	*II*	*III*	*I*	*II*	*III*
Casual Conversation	48 (57.83)	18 (21 69)	17 (20.48)	19 (50.00)	13 (34.21)	6 (15.79)
Seeking help for problems other than monetary need	44 (53.01)	12 (14.46)	27 (32.53)	19 (50.00)	8 (21.05)	11 (28.95)
Seeking monetary assistance	44 (53.01)	21 (25 30)	18 (21 69)	18 (47.37)	15 (39.47)	5 (13.16)
Discussing vital domestic problems in search of solution	33 (39.76)	13 (15.66)	37 (44.58)	19 (50.00)	8 (21.05)	11 (28.95)
Sharing personal joys and sorrows	34 (40.96)	11 (13.25)	38 (45.78)	20 (52.63)	14 (36.84)	4 (10.53)
Total	203	75	137	95	58	37

Reasons for personal contact	*Naidu*			*Harijan*			*Other castes*		
	I	*II*	*III*	*I*	*II*	*III*	*I*	*II*	*III*
Casual Conversation	17 (51 52)	11 (33.33)	5 (15.15)	14 (48.28)	11 (37.93)	4 (13.79)	27 (40.30)	15 (22.39)	25 (37.21)
Seeking help for problems other than monetary need	14 (42.42)	5 (15.15)	14 (42.42)	13 (44.83)	6 (20.69)	10 (34.48)	24 (35.82)	9 (13.43)	34 (50.75)
Seeking monetary assistance	10 (30.30)	13 (39.40)	10 (30.30)	13 (44.83)	10 (34.48)	6 (20.69)	19 (28.36)	9 (13.43)	39 (58.11)
Discussing vital domestic problems in search of solution	13 (39.40)	9 (27.27)	11 (33.33)	11 (37.93)	5 (17.24)	13 (44.83)	22 (32.83)	6 (8.96)	39 (58.21)
Sharing personal joys and sorrows	15 (45.45)	13 (39.40)	5 (15.15)	11 (37.93)	3 (10.34)	15 (51.73)	26 (38.80)	7 (10.45)	34 (50.75)
Total	69	51	45	62	34	48	118	46	171

or less similar in this respect, that is, a considerable percentage of the respondents (an average of 41.82 per cent of the Naidus and 42.76 per cent of the Harijans) prefer friends from their own castes for those purposes. The item "other castes" is not important for the discussion here as it consists of several castes constituting below seven per cent. Nevertheless the Mukkulathors and the Pillais are high in preferring friends from their castemen and the Naidus and the Harijans are moderate in this regard.

On the other hand, nearly one-third of the Pillais and the Naidus prefer friends from other castes for those purposes, whereas nearly one-fourth of the Harijans and more or less one-sixth of the Mukkulathors do so. This shows that the Pillais, Naidus and Harijans are low in preferring friends from other castes and the Mukkulathors are least in doing so.

However, it has been proved statistically that the correlation between caste of the respondents and their choice of friends for those purposes such as seeking monetary assistance and sharing personal joys and sorrows, is significant. But this correlation is found insignificant for other three purposes, that is, casual conversation, seeking help for problems other than monetary need and discussing vital domestic problems in search of solution. Thus, on the whole the correlation between the two variables are not uniformly significant for all the five purposes. This is shown Table 24.

In addition to this, an analysis of the relationship between the two variables in terms of the rural and urban background of the respondents, reveals a different pattern of relationship. This is shown Table 24.

On the whole, it is seen that the Harijan respondents in the two mills show significant variation with regard to their choice of friends for three purposes; the Mukkulathors do so for two purposes and the Pillais for only one purpose. But the Naidus in the mills do not show significant variation with regard to their choice of friends for all the five purposes. Thus the respondents from the Harijan and the Mukkulathor communities are moderate in preferring friends from their castemen; the Pillais are least in this matter and the Naidus do not

Table 23

Relationship between the Caste of Respondents and their Choice of Friends

Purpose of contact	*Chi-square*	*Degrees of freedom*	*P*
Casual conversation	15.255	8	P>0.05
Seeking help for problems other than monetary need	8.597	8	P>0.05
Seeking monetary assistance	39.134	8	P<0.05
Discussing vital domestic problems in search of solution	12.848	8	P>0.05
Sharing personal joys and sorrows	37.456	8	P<0.05

show significant variation in this.

In mill A, the respondents from the Harijan community come from their colonies situated in the neighbouring villages. Still they have inhibitions in preferring friends among their colleagues from other castes. Their choice of friend is more from among the colleagues of their caste than from among those belonging to other castes. But the Harijans in mill B live in the midst of Caste-Hindus in various residential areas in Madurai City. This has removed their inhabitions to a notable extent and made them move freely with the Caste-Hindus. This may be reason for the respondents in mill A preferring friends from among their castemen. On the contrary, the Harijan respondents in mill B prefer friends from other castes.

The Mukkulathors in mill A are the natives of neighbouring villages. As mentioned earlier in this chapter, they come to work daily in groups by bicycles or buses. This non-work situation promotes constant interaction among them. They are widely distributed in all the departments of the mill. So their choice of friends is more among the colleagues of their own caste. But in mill B, a majority of the respondents

Table 24

Relationship between the Background of Respondents from Different Castes and their Choice of Friends for Personal Contacts

Reasons for Contact	*Mukkulathor*	*Pillai*	*Naidu*	*Harijan*	*Other castes*
Casual conversation	5.212 (NS)	4.729 (NS)	0.000 (NS)	6.336 (S)	16.515 (S)
Seeking help for problems other than monetary need	5.828 (NS)	3.910 (NS)	3.394 (NS)	5.579 (NS)	14.070 (S)
Seeking monetary assistance	2.216 (NS)	1.058 (NS)	1.558 (NS)	4.300 (NS)	10.657 (S)
Discussing vital domestic problems in search of solutions	15.285 (S)	4.425 (NS)	1.076 (NS)	6.008 (S)	6.917 (S)
Sharing personal joys and sorrows	8.881 (S)	7.475 (S)	3.399 (NS)	6.236 (S)	1.322 (NS)

S: Significant at 0.05 level.
NS: Not significant.

(68 per cent) from the Mukkulathor caste come from residential areas situated adjacent to the mill. Since they live in the midst of a heterogeneous population, they make acquaintance with people from other castes too. They follow a similar practice in the mill. In other words, they make friends from other castes too. Thus, in mill B, the Mukkulathors' choice of friends is less among their castemen than among those from other castes. But in mill A, the Mukkulathors prefer to restrict their friendship to their own castemen. This results in significant difference between the background of the respondents in both the mills and their choice of friends for the last two purposes which are important for the development of intimate friendship.

In mill A, a majority of the respondents (58 per cent) from the Pillai caste and a large majority of the respondents (76 per cent) from the Naidu caste come from the neighbouring town, Melur. Since they live in the midst of a heterogeneous population, they move with people from various castes and make friends among them. This makes them follow such a trend in the mill too. Thus, generally, there is no significant relationship between the rural-urban backgrounds of the respondents from the Pillai and the Naidu castes on the one hand and their choice of friends for those purposes on the other hand.

The respondents who approach their colleagues for problems other than monetary need, like discussing vital domestic problems in search of solution and sharing joys and sorrows, consider them their intimate friends. A majority of respondents (an average of 57.65 per cent in mill A and 30.26 per cent in mill B) have their intimate friends from among their castemen. In other words, the respondents in mill A are more prone to caste considerations than those in mill B in the matter of making intimate friends. It is, therefore, evident that there is significant relationship between the background of the respondents and their choice of intimate friends.

The urban workers of mill B are scattered in different residential areas. They are exposed to different situations in which they meet people from varied cultural background. They interact with them for different reasons. In an urban environment such interaction has to cut across caste barriers. Thus the workers pick up acquaintance with persons from different castes. The canteen in mill B also brings them together. They have inter-dining here. Similarly the workers' quaters provided by mill B facilitate the interaction among the workers from different castes. But there are no such facilities in mill A. Consequently, the interaction among the respondents in rural mill is more caste-oiented than the interaction among those in urban mill.

Vasant Deshpande comes to similar conclusions on the observance of caste system in rural and urban areas. He notes that knowing the caste of a colleague becomes unimportant to a worker. The canteens in factories bring all workers together. There, a worker is so busy that he may not be interested to know about the caste of his colleague who sits next to him. The industrial atmosphere facilitates wider relationship among workers from different castes and helps the development of friendship among them.[4]

Interaction between the Workers and the Office Staff

The staff of the mills can be broadly classified into two divisions : main office staff and factory staff. The main office is a little away from the shopfloor so that the staff of this office are free from the noise of the machines. They are mostly non-technical as they are not directly involved in production. On the other hand, the factory office is close to the shopfloor. The staff of this office are mostly technical and they are directly related to production. The workers are more familiar with them than with the main office staff. Since they are directly related to the process of production, the workers meet them frequently. They meet the factory staff mostly in formal situations for reasons such as work load, leave, salary, Employees' State Insurance, over-time work, loan, workers' token, canteen token and other related matters.

4. Vasant Deshpande, *Towards Social Integration* (Poona ; Shubhada-Saraswat, 1978), pp. 114-115.

The workers move with particular members of the staff mostly in informal situations for their personal problems with the purpose of seeking their assistance. An attempt was made to find out whether caste influences the choice of the staff member by the respondents for solving their personal problems.

Table 25

Respondents by their First Choice of Staff for their Personal Problems

Mill	*No. of respondents whose choices are their own castemen*	*No. of respondents whose choices are only men from other castes*	*No. of respondents who do not meet staff*	*Total*
A	24 (24.49)	20 (20.41)	54 (55.10)	98 (100.00)
B	16 (10.53)	37 (24.34)	99 (65.13)	152 (100.00)
Total	40 (16.00)	57 (22.80)	153 (61.20)	250 (100.00)

$X^2=7.950$ df=2 $P<0.05$

It is clear that of 98.44 (44.9 per cent) respondents in mill A meet the staff for their personal problems; 53 (34.87 per cent) out of 152 respondents in mill B do so. Of the 44, a majority (24 of 54.54 per cent) of the respondents in mill A meet their own castemen with such missions, and sixteen (30.19 per cent) out of 53 respondents in mill B do so. It is evident from this that the choice of respondents in mill A is more from among their castemen than from those of other castes in mill B. Therefore, there is significant relationship between the respondents' choice of staff for their personal problems and their rural-urban background.

All the 97 (38.8 per cent) respondents of the two mills meet the staff both in the main office and in the factory. They were asked to give reasons for meeting their castemen in these offices. Of forty, 22 (55 per cent) respondents (thirteen in mill A and nine in mill B) frankly say that they approach them with the purpose of gaining their help because of caste relations; eleven (32.35 per cent) respondents (seven in mill A and four in mill B) report that they approach them as they reside in their locality; and seven (17.5 per cent) respondents (four in mill A and three in mill B) mention that since they are kind enough to attend to their problems, they approach them.

Nevertheless, a majority of the respondents (55.10 per cent in mill A and 65.13 per cent in mill B) say that they do not meet the staff for their personal problems. This is because they think that they are below the rank of the office staff. They say that they approach their departmental maistrys and their union leaders for any personal problems. It is inferred from this that they have a notion that they belong to a different category which is lower in status. They assume that it is a big thing on the part of a worker to meet the staff for personal problems.

Of seventeen (six in mill A and eleven in mill B), eight staff (two in mill A and six in mill B) approach either the officers or the managers who are kind and helpful to them. Of eight, four staff (one in mill A and three in mill B) approach their castemen who are responsible for their appointments. Other staff (nine) say that they do not approach the officers or the managers for their personal problem mainly because of the status difference.

Marxian thought posits three levels in the development of class consciousness : awareness of various segments in industrial organisations, awareness of the hierarchy in terms of high and low and awareness of their exploitation by those who are at the helm of affairs, that is, at the top of the hierarchy. Though we may think that the respondents who do not meet the staff for their personal problems seem to fit in the second level in the development of class consciousness explained by Marx, they are prevented by caste loyalties from forming a class for itself against the management.

Interaction between the Workers and the Maistrys

As the workers on shopfloor are under the direct control of the maistrys, they approach them for solving their problems concerning work. Moreover they interact more with the maistrys than with the leaders of their unions.

Maistrys in Mill A

There are six head maistrys in mill A supervising 916 workers. They are all promotees from the ranks of labour, and they have no special technical qualification making them specially suited to their job. Seniority, obedience and influence are all factors that weigh in the promotion of a worker to the position of a maistry.

Between maistry and worker, there are two other categories namely the oiler and the fitter. But theirs are not supervisory positions. These two think of themselves only as workers but the maistry does not. He is vested with great powers. He can be seen punishing the workers when he deems them wrong : levying fines, or even asking an erring worker to proceed on leave. The workers are afraid of him. At every stage they try to please him. In spite of these, a maistry is basically a worker who joins other workers in shopfloor. But he fails to sympathize with the problems of workers. Instead their interests lay in continuing to serve the interests of the management within the social relationship of production.

The maistrys thus exist as a group distinct from their subordinates. This is supported by a fact that they have separate union (Fitter, Maistry and Oiler Sangam) to get their problems solved. This union has no relationship with other labour unions. Since they have power and certain privileges, they do not identify themselves with the workers.

But the supervisory cadres do not accept them as of their rank. They feel too far above the maistrys because they are possessed of technical qualifications like the diploma in textile technology. The maistrys know that they are below in rank to their supervisors, though their advice and suggestions form the basis of the decisions of the supervisory staff. Thus the disinterestedness of the maistrys to identify themselves with the workers on the one hand and their inability to associate themselves with the supervisors on the other hand makes their position ambiguous. It is because of these reasons that Sheth sees in them the group that feels most deprived among the industrial worker-groups.

However, the caste relation is prominent in the interaction between the maistrys and the workers. The maistrys favour workers of their own caste, who come under their jurisdiction. Thus the evolution of a class spirit is hindered in this rural mill by distinctions in labour cadre and caste considerations.

Maistrys in Mill B

The position of maistrys in this mill is different. They do not think of themselves as a distinct group. Though they wield their power over the workers, they still know that they belong to the same cadre. For all practical purposes, they identify themselves with them. They do not have separate union for themselves. Instead they join various labour unions, participate in strikes and even take their problems to the union leaders. In other words, in this mill, they appear less as the establishment-men. The workforce in this mill is larger (1407) and there are ten head maistrys. It is observed that the relationship between maistrys and the workers is more cordial in mill B than in mill A. The maistrys in mill B do not feel that, in all occasions, they safeguard the interest of the management. Much of this cannot be proved with statistics but the differences is evident to an observer. Thus in this urban atmosphere small differences in cadre are not decisive forces of division.

Favouritism of Maistrys in the Mill

An attempt was made to find out whether the maistrys are helpful to employees of their caste who approach them for solving their problems arising out of their work, or for getting overtime work or seeking help for promotion. Opinions of respondents were obtained. It is found that the maistrys are indeed helpful to the employees of their own caste. The opinion of the employees regarding the favouritism of their immediate heads is shown in Table 26.

In mill A, 34.69 per cent of the respondents (including) three of the office staff in mill A and two in mill B) are of the view that their immediate heads favour the employees of their own caste. This is thrice as much as their counterparts (11.18 per cent) in mill B. The respondents who say that their immediate heads favour those providing monetary and non-monetary help are more or less same in the two mills. In mill B, the respondents who are applicable to both these categories are twice as many as those in mill A. It is evident that the favouritism is more pronounced among the immediate heads in mill A than their counterparts in mill B. There is thus significant relationship between rural-urban background of the immediate heads and their favouritism to their subordinates.

The investigator had an informal discussion with all the head maistrys of the two mills with a view to see whether in their opinion they favour workers of their own caste. Of sixteen, three maistrys (one in mill A and two in mill B) are included in the sample. The maistrys were asked to specify their treatment of the workers who come to them for obligations. Out of sixteen, five maistrys (two in mill A and three in mill B) say that they do the needful within their limits. Further they say that they have to be considerate to men of their own caste in certain situations; unless they are so, they could be blamed by their castemen who normally expect such favours from them. But the other maistrys say that they are helpful to all the workers working in their departments.

There is an apparent anomaly in this Table. It is that caste considerations appear to play a lesser role in the interaction between the maistrys and the workers particularly with respect to the maistrys' helpful attitude to the workers. But this can be explained on the basis of certain case studies by the investigator. The case studies reveal that many of the workers irrespective of their caste go all out to please the

Table 26

Respondents by their Opinions regarding the Favouritism of their Immediate Heads

Mill	*Favourable castemen*	*Favourablc to those who extend their help*	*Both*	*Neutral*	*No idea*	*Total*
A	34 (34.69)	15 (15.31)	8 (8.16)	38 (38.78)	3 (3 06)	98 (100.00)
B	17 (11.18)	19 (12.50)	30 (19.74)	79 (51.97)	7 (4.61)	152 (100.00)
Total	51 (20.40)	34 (13.60)	38 (15.20)	117 (46.80)	10 (4.00)	250 (100.00)

$X^2=24.724$ df=4 $P<0.05$

maistrys and curry their favour, getting coffee or tea or alcoholic drinks for them, doing menial service, presenting vegetables, and even offering cash. That is why the maistrys' helpful attitude within the industrial context is not only oriented to their castemen but also to men from other castes.

Thus the caste relation is notable in the two mills. However, in different interacting situations the polarization of employees towards caste is more in rural mill than in the urban mill. This variation may be attributed to the differences in the features of workforce in rural and urban areas. Yet this does not mean that the workforce in the urban mill cuts across the caste barriers in order to form a class truly for class action.

The workforce in both the mills virtually forms a class which in the Marxian terminology is a "class in itself". But the caste loyalties predominate to the extent that they prevent the development of class consciousness to the extent of forming a "class for itself".

6

Trade Union

A trade union is a legitimate and voluntary association of employees in industrial organisations. Such associations are supposed to be formed to protect and advance the common interests of employees arising from their common experiences in relation to their employment. These associations may also have a set of common objectives that they may want to achieve as employees. Sheth mentions that the common interests of trade union members can often be articulated in economic terms such as improvement in wage rates, fringe benefits, incentive or welfare measures. At the same time, a large number of union objectives may relate to non-economic issues such as redressal of workers' grievance against management, promotion of their status as employees and citizens and resistance to what workers might regard as unreasonable exercise of management authority.[1] The common interests of the members are thus responsible for the formation of trade unions.

According to Sheth, the functions of a trade union are:

(i) helping members in the process of articulation and

1. N.R. Sheth, "Trade Union in Social Reality," in *Industrial Relations in India*, ed. E.A. Ramaswami (Delhi: Macmillan, 1976), pp. 64-68.

expression of their common interests;

(ii) acting as an agency through which these common interests are protected and promoted;

(iii) generating and reinforcing among the members the consciousness of common experience and interest; and

(iv) like other interest-groups, helping their members to achieve the status of citizens in the industry as well as in society.[2]

A trade union is a formal organisation. Its hierarchy broadly consists of two levels: Members and office bearers. Ishwar Dayal and Sharma mention that the workers' reason for joining a union seems to be negative, that is, exploitation by the management, whereas the motive for becoming a leader is positive, that is, to serve the workers. The two motives, however, seem to reinforce each other.[3] The authority of union leaders is derived from members who are closely involved in union affairs. At the same time, they exercise their authority over the membere. For instance, leaders are expected to guide members regarding the quantum of wage rise to be demanded, the timing of demands, when a strike should be called, at what stage it should be withdrawn and so on. In exercising authority over members on such matters, leaders cannot neglect the fact that members can easily withdraw their support to the union by refusing to pay union dues and to participate in union activities. Union finances are subject to uncertainties arising out of the members' discretion with regard to payment of dues and the efficiency of those who collect union dues. Union leaders, therefore, tend to work under conditions of relative insecurity.[4]

The main function of the union leader is to negotiate the demands of the members with the management and take

2. Sheth, "Trade Union in Social Reality," p. 65.
3. Ishwar Daval and B.R. Sharma, *Management of Trade Unions* (New Delhi: Sri Ram Centre for Industrial Relations and Human Resources, 1976),.p. 52.
4. Sheth, "Trade Union in Social Reality," pp. 68-69.

legally recognised and permissible steps to get what they want. Sheth points out that union leaders become a part of the management to a certain extent as they collaborate with it concerning to shopfloor issues relating to productivity, safety, discipline or grievance. The leaders' attitude tends to become similar to that of the management. They tend to be "psychologically absorbed by (the) management."[5]

Generally, trade unions are absent in handicraft industries. For instance, there are no trade unions in the diamond industry studied by Kalathil. He finds that wages and conditions of work in this industry are not subject to collective bargaining, arbitration or adjudication. It does not mean that there are no disputes among these workers or between them and their employees. There are disputes, but there are also ways to solve them without resorting to formal procedure.[6]

But big establishments bringing together a large number of workers tend to have a number of unions. In modern time, thanks to the strength that numbers command, all political parties tend to be very much—often too much—interested in trade unions. The tensions and conflicts in the political world are reflected in the world of trade unions also. Thus big organizations tend to have a multiplicity of trade unions. As caste is pervasive reality of India's social organization, workers also tend to be united under the banner of caste-oriented organizations. Thus the world of trade unions is invaded by caste considcrations which are strictly speaking extraneous to the workers' world. There are unions explicity calling themselves by the name of their caste persuasions, and even where this is not the case, these interests tend to be latent forces in union organizations.

In both the mills selected for the present study, the workers have formed several trade unions affiliated to different political parties. This chapter tries to study the working of trade unions and the influence of caste and class relations on these. Such a study is bound to throw light on the workers' attitude towards their union and union leaders.

5. Ibid., pp. 72-73.
6. Ibid., p. 73.

The trade unions in both the mills are listed below:

1. The PTMS—Panchalai Thozhilalar Sangam (affiliated to the Dravide Munnetra Kazhagam).
2. The ATS—Anna Thozhilalar Sangam (affiliated to the All India Anna Dravide Munnetra Kazhagam).
3. The INTUC—Indian National Trade Union Congress (affiliated to the Congress-I).
4. The HMS—Hind Mazdoor Sabha (No party affiliation, but sympathises with the Congress-I).
5. The AITUC—All India Trade Union Congress. This is locally known as MDUPTS—Madurai District United Panchalai Thozhilalar Sangam (affiliated to the Communist Party of India).
6. CITU—Centre for Indian Trade Union [affiliated to the Communist Party of India (Marxist)].
7. The MTC—Mill Thozhilalar Congress (affiliated to the Janatha).
8. The UFFR—United Front Federation of Repatriates (No party affiliation).
9. The FMOS—Fitter, Maistry, Oiler Sangam (No party affiliation).

In addition to this, the office staff of the two mills have associations for their welfare. But they are ineffective as the members are not interested in association activities. Table 27 shows the distribution of respondents according to different unions and associations.

In mill A, about one-fourth (27.55 per cent) of respondents belong to the PTMS; in mill B, a high percentage (36.18) of respondents belong to the INTUC. In mill A, the ATS and the INTUC occupy the second and third places respectively leaving fourth and fifth places to the UFFR and the HMS respectively with regard to strength of the respondents. In mill B, the DMK, the HMS and the ATS are in the second, third and fourth places respectively. It is understood that the unions such as the AITUC, the CITU, the MTC and

Table 27

Respondents by Union/Association

Union	*Mill*	*Mukkulathor*	*Pillai*	*Naidu*	*Harijan*	*Other caste*	*Total*
PTMS	A	7	6	2	6	6	27(27.55)
	B	14	1	4	3	5	27(17.77)
ATS	A	4	2	2	3	5	16(16.33)
	B	6	3	3	1	1	14(9.21)
INTUC	A	4	2	2	3	4	15(15.31)
	B	19	10	8	6	12	55(36.18)
AITUC	A	1	1	—	—	1	3(3.06)
	B	5	2	—	—	3	10(6.58)
CITU	A	1	1	—	—	1	3(3.06)
	B	2	—	—	—	1	3(1.97)
MTC	A	1	—	—	—	1	2(2.04)
	B	2	1	2	—	1	6(3.95)
HMS	A	2	2	1	—	3	8(8.16)
	B	3	1	6	—	5	15(9.87)
UFFR	A	2	1	—	5	4	12(12.25)
	B	—	—	—	—	—	— —

FMOS	A	1	—	—	2	3	6(6.12)
	B	—	—	—	—	—	— —
Members in	A	—	—	—	—	—	— —
two unions	B	3	1	—	—	2	6(3.95)
No	A	—	—	—	—	—	— —
membership	B	3	—	2	—	—	5(3.29)
Staff	A	2	2	—	—	2	6(6.12)
Association	B	1	2	1	—	7	11(7.23)
	A	25	17	7	19	30	98(100.00)
Total	B	58	21	26	10	37	152(100.00)

the FMOS in both the mills constitute less than seven per cent of the respondents.

It is interesting to note that six respondents in mill B are members in two unions. According to them, they could seek help of both the unions to solve their problems in the mill. It is shown that all the seventeen staff in the mills are members in staff associations.

All the nine unions are represented in mill A. Four of them, namely, the PTMS, the UFFR, the ATS and the TNTUC, are powerful unions. They are recognized by the management.[7] They occupy the first, second, third and fourth places respectively as far as their numerical strength is concerned. They are capable of influencing the management in certain matters relating to labour. The settlements regarding labour problems are arrived at only after getting the official concurrence of the leaders of these powerful unions. But all other unions (AITUC, CITU, MTS and HMS) are not recognized by the management because they are minority in terms of their numerical strength, They are, therefore, categorised as powerless unions.

The first seven unions are represented in mill B. Three of them, the INTUC, the PTMS and the HMS, are powerful. They occupy first, second and third places in respect of numerical strength. They exercise more influence over the management in many matters concerning labour than their counterparts in mill A. The management takes decisions with regard to labour problems only after discussing them with the leaders of these unions. Thanks to this privilege, they demand certain things for their own benefit as well as the betterment of workers. If the management does not accept their demands, they persuade them in such a way as to get their demands fulfilled at least partially. Such privilege is not given to the leaders of the powerful unions in mill A. The Managing Director of the mill, an IAS officer, considers only the "genuine" demands of the leaders in general. But he does

7. It is usual practice of the mill managements that they establish affable relationship with numerically dominant unions anticipating their support at the time of labour unrest. Such unions are known as recognised unions in the mills.

not favour even the leaders of the powerful unions to fulfil their demands concerning personal benefits. On the contrary, the management of mill B is always favourable to the leaders of the powerful unions as it seeks their help for the settlement of the labour problems.

The reason is that mill A falls under the co-operative sector. The Managing Director does not consult the leaders of the powerful unions on all matters concerning labour, as he strictly follows the rules formulated by the Tamil Nadu Government for such mill all over the state. He neither favours these leaders unduly to get their support during the time of strike nor invites them for all discussions concerning workers' problems. On the other hand, the management of mill B which is privately owned angles for the support of the powerful unions by extending favours to their leaders. As a result, these leaders are invited by the management to all the discussions with regard to the workers' problem. Thus, the leaders exert influence over the management.

It is relevant in this context to discuss the characteristic features of the leaders. Murphy says that a typical Indian worker-leader is generally an upper Caste-Hindu, older, better educated, politically more aware, a hard worker and usually a nationalist supporter.[8] However, except two, other characteristic features are not applicable to the union leaders in the mills studied. The characteristic features such as education and political awareness are applicable to the union leaders in the present study, but the others are not applicable to them.

The average age of the union leaders in mill A is 40, whereas it is 45 in mill B. In both cases, they are middle-aged persons. In both the mills, the number of union leaders (about 50 per cent in each mill) from the lower rung of the caste hierarchy is more or less balanced by those (about 50 per cent in each mill) from the upper rung. All are Hindus except three, two Christians and a Muslim. All of them in mill A have had an average of ten years of schooling as against their counterparts in mill B who have had seven years of schooling. This may be accounted for by the fact that in mill B, the

8. Murphy, *Unions in Conflict*, p. 92.

leaders whose age range is 37 to 55 joined as workers much earlier than those in the range 34 to 47 in mill A. According to the concerned shift supervisors, four leaders (two from each mill) are hard workers. Seven leaders (four in mill A and three in mill B) are migrants.

An attempt was made to study the influence of caste and class relations in trade unions by dividing the unions into two categories one consisting of Communist unions and the other of non-Communist unions. Generally, it is inferred from the present study that caste relations in Communist unions is more or less insignificant, but it is significant in non-Communist unions. Conversely, class relations is insignificant in non-Communist unions, but significant to a limited extent in Communist unions. This is discussed in the first half of this chapter.

Crouch finds that caste does not play any role in Indian trade unions irrespective of their affiliation to Communist or non-Communist parties. He observes, "trade union leaders with whom I have spoken almost universally claimed that caste and communal factors play no part in trade unionism."[9] However, in the present study, it is seen in the non-Communist unions that there is a relationship between numerical strength of castes and their representation in union leadership. In other words, a caste consisting of a majority or fairly high percentage of members in a union brings its man to power. This is shown Table 28.

The same relationship is shown in Table 29 with help of figures.

In mill A, the Mukkulathors, the Pillais and the Naidus have leadership positions in accordance with their numerical strength. The Mukkulathors have occupied leadership position twenty-three times. Though the Pillais are in the second place with regard to their strength, they occupy the third place in terms of the frequency of union leadership. But the Naidus whose numerical strength is less than that of the Pillais, occupy the second place. The reason is that in the ATS the

9. Harold Crouch, *Trade Unions and Politics in India* (Bombay: Manaktalas, 1966), p. 22.

Table 28

Dominant Caste in the Unions and their Representation to Union Leadership

Union	*Mill*	*Caste/s dominating the union in terms of numerical strength*	*Caste/s representing union leaders*
Non-Communist union			
PTMS	A	Mukkulathor and Pillai	Mukkulathor and Pillai
	B	Mukkulathor and Naidu	Mukkulathor and Naidu
ATS	A	Mukkulathor, Naidu and Pillai	Mukkulathor, Naidu and Pillai
	B	Naidu and Mukkulathor	Naidu and Mukkulathor
INTUC	A	Mukkulathor, Pillai and Harijan	Mukkulathor, Naidu and other Castes
	B	Mukkulathor and Naidu	Mukkulathor and Naidu
HMS	A	Pillai and Mukkulathor	Pillai and Mukkulathor
	B	Mukkulathor and Naidu	Mukkulathor and Naidu
MTC	A	Mukkulathor and Harijan	Mukkulathor and other Castes
	B	Mukkulathor and Naidu	Mukkulathor and Naidu
UFFR	A	Harijan	Other Castes
	—		
FMOS	A	Mukkulathor and Naidu	Mukkulathor
Communist union			
AITUC	A	Harijan	Harijan
	B	Mukkulathor and Pillai	Other Castes
CITU	A	Pillai	Other Castes
	B	Mukkulathor and Harijan	Other Castes

Table 29

Frequencies of Union Leadership Positions in the Mills by their Castes

Caste	*Numerical strength of caste at labour level*		*Frequency of union leadership*	
	Mill A	*Mill B*	*Mill A*	*Mill*
Mukkulathor	236 (25.16)	573 (40.73)	23	19
Naidu	59 (6.44)	256 (18.19)	11	10
Pillai	150 (17.04)	188 (13.36)	10	3
Harijan	188 (20.52)	98 (6.97)	1	—
Other Castes	277 (30.24)	292 (20.75)	14	9
Total	916 (100.00)	1407 (100.00)	—	--

Naidus are in a dominant position. As a result, in that union they have been in power since 1978.

On the other hand, the Mukkulathors, the Naidus and the Pillais in mill B occupy first, second and third places respectively with regard to their numerical strength. This is reflected in the union leadership too. It is clear that there is a direct relationship between the numerical strength of the castes and their representation in union leadership, especially in non-Communist unions. A person becomes a union leader if his caste commands a majority or consists of fairly high percentage of members in the union. It is evident that caste plays a vital role in the election of leaders in non-Communist unions. Generally, the members of a dominant caste in a union do not like men from other castes coming to power. This trend is observed in those unions. Certain interesting cases in both the mills are discussed here.

In mill A, a leader of the PTMS explains:

> I belong to the Konar caste. The Mukkulathors who constitute one-third of the population in the union did not like me to contest for the president's post. But I contested in the election with the support of other castes. I defeated my opponent who belonged to the Kallar community. Taking this as a prestige issue, he often troubled me. Similarly another Kallar who was the first president of the union opposed my decisions in the union meetings with a view to insult me. For instance, in the previous meeting, he seriously opposed my suggestions with regard to workers' problems. However, I left the decision to the executive committee. A majority of them accepted my suggestions.
>
> The Kallars want to push me down. As I am honest and sincere in my work, they do not succeed in their attempts. Since the Kallars and the Pillais of the union are numerically stronger, they have come to an understanding that if the Kallars recommend one of their castemen to contest for the secretary's post, the Pillais can recommend their candidates for the president's post. These two castes have been monopolizing the union ever since its inception.

In mill B, the Mukkulathors dominate the PTMS. They do not like men from other castes to be the leader. The present president and secretary of the union belong to the Mukkulathor caste.

A similar trend is found in the ATS of mill A. The present secretary of the union is a Naidu. He explains his problems thus:

> I defeated a Pillai in the recent union election. Consequently, he turned against me. Even today he is a problem to me. He is a trouble monger also to the union president who is a Naidu. He often opposes our

suggestions in the union meetings. He incites his castemen to counter us. Like the Pillais, the Kallars do not support us.

This is confirmed by the information collected from three Kallar and two Pillai respondents. They openly say that they want to remove the leaders from the Naidu caste from power. They also want to bring their candidates to power. Since one-third of the union members belong to the Kallar division of the Mukkulathor caste, they want to dominate the union. Though the Naidus are only next to the Kallars with regard to strength in the union, they dominate over the Kallars. They want to retain the power. Thus there is a power struggle between the Kallars and the Naidus in the union.

But the ATS in mill B shows a different picture. As regards this union, there is no intra-union conflict but there is inter-union conflict. This union was started in 1972 by a Naidu. He says that he was constantly troubled by the leaders of the powerful unions such as the INTUC, the PTMS and the HMS. For instance, in 1977, he wanted to discuss with the management an increase in the bonus. Before that, he had an informal discussion with the leaders of those unions. They pretended to support his demand. As proposed, he met the management.

Since the management did not want to increase the percentage of bonus, it turned down his demand. After that, the leaders of those powerful unions met the management on the same issue. They accepted the percentage of bonus already fixed by the management. This put the secretary of the ATS in an embarrassing situation. Later he came to know that those leaders pretended to support his view mainly to create a bad impression about him among the employers. From his viewpoint, they do not want him to become a powerful leader like them.

He narrates another instance which was responsible for his dismissal from the secretary's post. In 1982, he prepared a demand chart in consultation with the executive committee and other knowledgeable members of his union. He wanted to submit it to the management with the intention to make the management recognize his union. Before that, he gained the support of other unions such as the MTC, the AITUC and the CITU. But the leaders of the three powerful unions did not like this because they never wanted the ATS union to become equally powerful. They strongly criticized his move. They complained to the management about his attempt. They also urged the management to take action against him. Taking them into confidence, the management wrote to the founder president of the AIADMK against the secretary of the union. After a few days, he was dismissed from the post by the high command of the party. A worker from the Konar caste succeeded to his position with the help of one of the AIADMK leaders who was also a Konar.

In all the three powerful unions in mill A and mill B, the Mukkulathors, the Pillais and the Naidus are numerically dominant. However, the present leaders of these unions except INTUC and ATS in mill A belong to the Mukkulathor caste. Always there is a power struggle among the three castes in these unions. Since the establishment of ATS in mill B, the Naidus have been the dominant caste leaving next place to the Mukkulathors. It is understood from the discussion with the founder secretary of the union that he was not troubled by the Mukkulathors in his union. Instead, the leaders of the powerful unions joined together to put him in trouble. They prevented him from becoming a powerful leader like them as they feared that he would easily become a popular leader in the mill by gaining the support of his political party which was the then ruling party.

Though this is a valid reason inferred from the discussion with the leader of the ATS, the rivalry between him and the leaders of the powerful unions is partly attributed to their caste rivalry. As already discussed in Chapter III, the Mukkulathors and the Naidus in mill B are rivals. The instigation of management which is to be discussed later, is also an important reason for such rivalry.

It is important to note that though the other unions are not free from caste influence, they do not have such a problem arising out of inter-union conflicts. The problems of those unions are mostly caused by intra-union conflict. Such conflicts are the result of caste rivalries among the workers. Generally, such rivalries are caused by competition for power between two castes with more or less equal power in the union.

In addition to this, the management policy of 'divide and rule' seems to be an important cause of the inter-union conflicts which have their root in caste rivalry. It is understood from both the incidents narrated by the founder of ATS that the attempts of the leaders of the powerful unions to suppress him were deliberate and perhaps motivated by the management. Though there are no data to support this, an observer may arrive at a similar conclusion by carefully examining the inter-union conflicts. Thus the instigation of the management in such conflicts also curtails the unity of workers in order to keep them away from labour-management dispute. In such circumstances, the workers may not emerge as a powerful force against the management and hence the absence of class consciousness.

The leaders of the PTMS, the INTUC, the HMS, the MTC and the FMOS in the two mills are mostly represented by the majority castes in these unions. The caste relations in the union is very much realized. But, in the UFFR of mill A, the members who are Tamil Repatriates of Sri Lanka seem to be uninterested in caste relations. All the respondents of this category uniformly say that they do not give importance to caste affiliations. They also say that they were outside the caste-fold while living in Sri Lanka for several years. They were brought up there in such a way as to ignore the caste of their own and the others. Similarly, they are least concerned with the caste of other workers in the mill. At the time of data-collection, a few of them were reluctant to tell their castes. However, the investigator collected the information pertaining to this from their maistrys. A majority of them (51.26 per cent) belong to the Harijan community leaving second place to the Mukkulathor caste. It is observed that they move freely with the workers from other castes. They are well united and helpful to one another. For instance, in the case of death or marriage in one of their families, all the repatriates apply for mass casual leave. But this has become a problem to the management as the production is affected to a considerable extent. So it has passed an order stating that the workers as a whole or a section of them should not apply for casual leave on the same day. But this has not produced the expected result. Such a trend is not found among the workers from the other castes.

A Repatriate who is a worker from the Harijan community organised the UFFR union in 1978 with the support of all the 237 Tamil Repatriates in the mill. Before that they were members of the other unions of the mill. Though the founder of the union is a Harijan, the first president and the secretary of the union are from the Gounder caste and the Kallar division of the Mukkulathor caste respectively. They were elected by the members. They continued to be the leaders of the union for three years. There is no specific reason for their not electing a leader from the Harijan community which constitutes the majority of the union. The Harijans support their leaders in all respects. Hence the absence of intra-union rivalry.

It is interesting to find that only one Harijan is a leader in the AITUC of mill A. Except him no Harijan contested in union elections. Nearly one-third of the Harijan respondents in mill A say that they would like to contest in union elections, but their aspirations remain a day-dream. Conversely their counterparts in mill B do not like to contest for the reason that the workers from other castes do not like it.

It is relevant in this context to refer to Murphy's view that a typical worker leader is generally, an upper Caste-Hindu. Generally, the lower castes especially the Adi-Dravidas are not represented in the higher cadres. It would be much easier for higher caste persons to assume the leadership role, especially in the early stages of industrialization. The present study also shows a more or less similar trend. In both the mills, none of the Harijans, except one, occupies any leadership position (president or secretary or treasurer) in the unions.

One Harijan respondent in mill A explains thus his inability to contest in union elections:

> In 1980, I wanted to contest for the secretary's post. But later I dropped the idea for the reason that the Caste-Hindus opposed it. They would not tolerate a Harijan becoming a union secretary. They have a strong feeling that they should not go after the Harijans for any obligation as they think it is infra dig to them. Once I happened to overhear a discussion among the Caste-Hindus in the union with regard to union election. They uniformly accepted the view that they should not allow the Harijans to contest in union elections. One Caste-Hindu says: "It will be a shame if we follow a Harijan (*Nam oru paraiyan pinnāl povathā* !)" If this is the situation, how can I contest in union election ?

Anouther Harijan respondent in mill A gives the following reason for not contesting union elections:

> Though I would like to contest in the union election for the president's post, I am unable to do so because of my social position. I do not have the experience of moving with learned persons and officials. So I feel unequal to the task of approaching top officials in the mill. In case I become a leader of the union, I will have to meet them frequently to discuss labour problems. I have to solve such problems then and there. If I am unable to solve the members' problems, they will abuse me and even put me in a critical situation. For these reasons, I do not want to contest for leadership position.

In the INTUC of mill A, the Mukkulathors and the Harijans individually consititute one-fourth of the members. A young Harijan who was an active member in the union explains his disappointment:

> In 1979, I was a very active member in the union. The leaders of the union (president and secretary) trusted me in all respects. They also assigned me all confidential work with regard to the union. They wanted me to contest in the union election for the president's post. I

myself had the intention to become a leader of the union. So, I revealed my plan to the union members in order to know their opinion. The Caste-Hindus who constitute the majority did not like my plan. They openly expressed their dissatisfaction over this. I was sure that I would win the election with the support of the members of my caste and a few members from other castes. However, I gave up my plan because I knew that the Caste-Hindus do not accept me as their leader. After this incident, I became an inactive member in the union.

In the same union, the Kallars, the Pillais and the Harijans individually constitute more or less one-fourth of the membership. Usually either a Kallar or a Pillai contests for the secretary's post. Since the Kallars and the Pillais are the powerful castes in the union, they have a dispute as to which community must contest in the union election especially for the secretary's post. They have now come to an agreement that each caste can recommed its candidate for the post. But winning the election by one of them depends on the support of the Harijans. At the time of election, both the Kallars and the Pillais plead with the Harijans to support their candidate.

In the last election, a Naidu was able to gain the support of the Harijans by promising them that he would help one of them to become an office-bearer in the next term. Consequently, he won the election and became the secretary of the union. But he could not keep his promise. This was resented by the Harijans. They decided that they should not support him in the next election.

This Naidu with whom the investigator had an informal discussion plainly says that the union members who often blame him are the Harijans. He also admits that he was unable to fulfil their demands as a majority of the union members did not like Harijans to come to power. It is therefore evident that the Harijans in mill A have no chance of becoming the union leaders except in the AITUC.

Though the Harijans in mill B do not have inhibitions against contesting union elections to the extent that their counterparts have in mill A, they do not like to contest in the elections. The reason is that the Caste-Hindus especially the Mukkulathors, the Pillais and the Naidus do not allow a Harijan to become a leader of their union. One Harijan reports:

> We are numerically fewer; if any one of us contests in the election, the members from other castes do not support him. Especially, the Mukkulathors would vigorously oppose us if we set up our candidate in the union election.

All the ten respondents from the Harijan community express more or less a similar view. On the contrary, Uma Ramaswamy who studied textile workers in Coimbatore city observes: "Many mill level union branches are headed by Harijans who admit that union activities are by and large free from caste prejudices."[10] In Coimbatore, there are many textile mills providing jobs to thousands of persons. A majority of the workforce in the city is from textile mills. The employment saturation in the city has brought about changes in the working atmosphere as well as the social life of the workers. Caste relations have been ignored to a notable extent. This provides opportunity for certain mill workers from the Harijan community in Coimbatore to become union leaders. This has not yet happened in Madurai and its vicinity.

But the Communist unions in both the mills show a different picture. In the mills, becoming a secretary of a Communist union does not normally depend on the numerical strength of castes. The Pillais and the Harijans in mill A and the Mukkulathors and the Harijons in mill B constitute a fairly high percentage of members in the Communist unions such as the AITUC and the CITU. However, most of the *office-bearers* of these unions belong to other castes. For instance, in the CITU of mill A, the Pillais constitute one-fourth of the members. The other castes such as the Kallar,

10. Uma Ramaswamy, *Worker, Union and Community*, p. 106.

the Moopanar and the Harijan individually constitute about sixteen per cent of the members. In spite of this caste composition, a Sourashtra has been the secretary of the union for four terms. But the numerical strength of the Sourashtras in the union is very low, that is, 4 71 per cent.

A few respondents in the union were asked to explain specifically as to how the Sourashtra continues to be the secretary of the union for four terms. They say that he is a knowledgeable leader. He is sincere in union activities. He is polite to everyone in the union. He attends to the problems of the workers immediately. So the union members do not object his continuing as the secretary. This does not mean that they are free from caste loyalties.

The investigator had a brief discussion with the leader in order to learn the commitment of the members to the union. He says that except a few, the members have neither union participation nor political involvement at the higher level, but they have caste considerations to a notable extent. This is evident from an incident narrated by him.

> The numerical strength of our union was more than a hundred in 1980. After that there was a decrease in the strength of the union. The leader and a few active members from other unions incited many members of the CITU to join their unions on caste lines. As a result, one-third of the members left the CITU and joined other unions according to the numerical strength of their caste members in such unions. The increase of membership in a union depends on the numerical strength of different castes in the union.

Unlike the leader of the CITU, the leader of the AITUC belongs to the Harijan community which constitute the majority (about 60 per cent). Since 1975 the Harijans have been joining the mill in large numbers. They continue to occupy second place with regard to numerical strength. Encouraged by this, an enthusiastic Harijan worker started the AITUC in 1978 with the help of his castemen. He continues to be the secretary of the union for three terms successively.

The Harijans are dominant in the union. Since the individual strength of other castes in the union is below seven per cent, they neither object to his continuing as secretary nor contest in union elections. However, they are members in one of the powerful unions too.

It is important to note that the workers in this union from the Mukkulathor, the Pillai and the Naidu castes are very few in number. The dominant position of the Harijans and the numerical minority of other castes in the unions are the main reasons for giving rise to the practice of changing the membership from one union to another. But the problem of dual membership is found among the members in the two Communist unions.

As far as the caste composition of the CITU in mill B is concerned, the Mukkulathors and the Harijans individually constitute nearly one-third of the population. However, the secretary of the CITU in this mill was a Konar. He was a committed Communist. But the employers of the mill did not recognize his union. They wanted to dismiss him from the mill. In 1981, the textile workers at the All India level called for a token strike for a day. The non-Communist unions especially the powerful unions in mill B did not want to participate in the strike. But the two Communist unions in the mill planned to stop the production on that day. The leader of the CITU was especially active in this. The leaders of the powerful unions opposed his move because the management had sought their help in advance to break this strike. While approaching the workers in the early hours of the day to stop production, the CITU leader was assaulted by a few members of the powerful unions. Immediately a few policemen entered the shopfloor and arrested the leader along with a few members of his union. It was the view of a few respondents that the whole thing was planned by the management to trap the leader. Consequently, the leader was suspended from the mill. A case was also filed against him and other members of his union alleging that they tried to assault some of the workers who refused to stop production. In his absence, the union became inactive. A few members of the union report that their leader was likely to be reinstated soon.

This incident supports thc finding again that the management is, like caste, a crucial divider of workers into hostile groups in the pretext of labour discipline. In addition to this, management finds multi-unionism as a favourable ground to promote union rivalries in order to get economic benefits and also prevent the workers from the attempt of uniting together for class action. This is substantiated by the finding ot Ramachandra Raj. He observes: "Multi-unionism among the labour tends to transfer every rational economic conflict between management and labour into one of inter-union in which the management tends to derive economic benefits and advantage over the labour by forging and alliance with one section of the labour."[11]

Irrespective of caste, all the respondents from the CITU say that their leader is efficient, sincere and helpful to everyone in the union. They uniformly want him to continue to be their leader. It seems that the members of the union do not follow caste affiliations. But, it is not that the members of this union are highly involved in the Communist party. Except a few the members of the union have neither union participation nor political involvement at the higher level.

The secretary of the AITUC says that his union is not based on caste relations. He himself does not know the caste of the members of his union. Persons from the Pillai, the Konar, the Mukkulathor and the Muthuraja communities have been successive secretaries. Union elections are not based on caste considerations. The secretary refers to his own case as an example. Though there are only ten workers in the mill belonging to his caste, he has been the secretary of the mill for more than fifteen years. This is so because he is highly committed to the principles of the party. The party leaders also want him to continue to be the secretary of the union. So there is no caste influence either in the union election or in its activities. He says that only one-fourth of the respondents in the union are committed to the principles of the party and the union.

11. Ramachandra Raj, *In the content of conflicts in the larger system: A study of industrial conflict in Kerala*, pp. 76-77.

In the Communist unions of mill A and mill B, the presidents are outsiders. They are the presidents of all such unions in Madurai District. But the presidents of non-Communist unions are elected from among workers in the mills. Mostly the secretaries of Communist unions in the mills belong to a minority caste in the unions as well as in the mills. They continue to be the secretaries of the unions for several years without opposition from the members of the dominant castes. One reason for this is that the leaders are highly committed to the principles of their party. They are sincere and honest. They attend to the problems of the members without expecting either monetary benefit or other kinds of return or reward. They have a sense of involvement in attending to the problem of every individual member or the problem of the union as a whole.

On the other hand, the leaders of the non-Communist unions cannot be the leaders for years together. Occasionally a few leaders continue to maintain their position for two or three terms. However, in most of the unions, this does not happen because of the power struggle between two dominant castes. The leaders who are caste-minded, selfish and corrupt may lose support of the members. They would not become leaders again.

The managements in the two mills do not want to establish relationship with the powerless (Communist and non-Communist) unions which in turn do not want to be their supporters. There is, therefore, a strained relationship between them. On the contrary, there is a cordial relationship between the managements and the powerful (non-Communist) unions. Similarly, a warm relationship between the managements on the one hand and the Fitter, Maistry, Oiler Sangam (FMOS) and the Staff Associations (SA) on the other, is prevalent in the mills. This is so because the leaders of the FMOS and the SA are always the supporters of the managements. It is found that there is a common understanding among the leaders of the powerless unions as found among their counterparts in the powerful unions. But the relationship between the powerful and powerless unions is hostile. The figure on page 149 shows the relationship between the manage-

FIGURE-2

UNION MANAGEMENT RELATIONSHIP AND

INTER AND INTER-UNION RELATIONSHIP

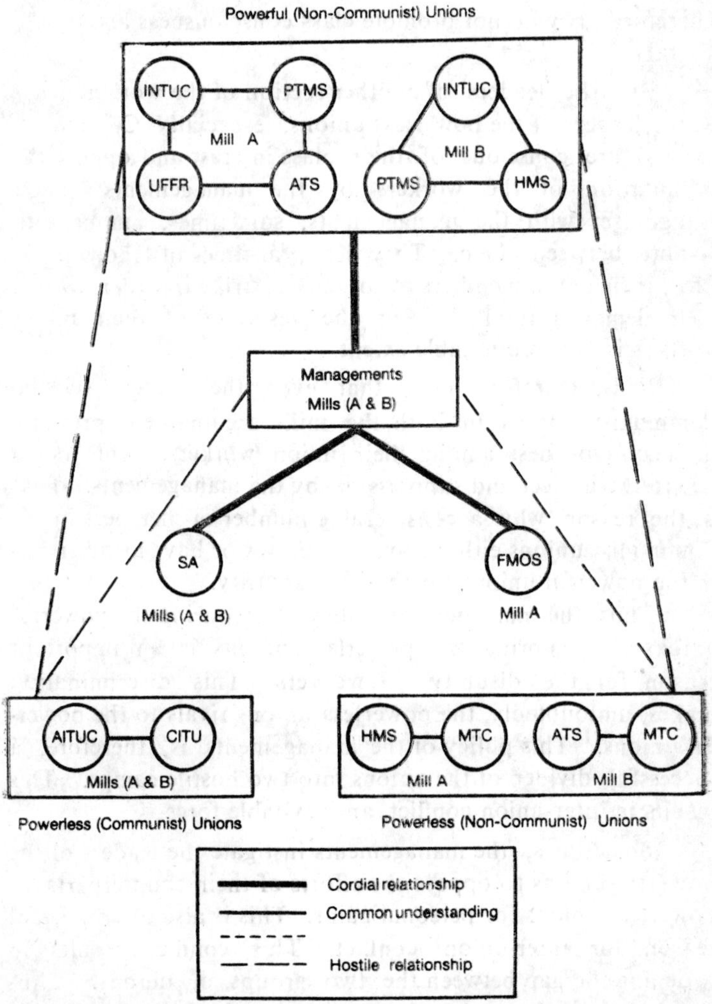

ments and the unions on the one hand and the relationship among the unions on the other.

The multi-unionism in the mills tends to become dichotomous. The leaders of one section of the workers (that is, the leaders of the powerful unions) have become tools of the managements mostly for personal gains. They are not aware of their class in opposition to the managements. Therefore, they do not promote class consciousness among the workers.

But the leaders of another section of the workers (that is, the leaders of the powerless unions, especially Communist unions) are conscious of their class interest and oppose the exploitation of the workers by the managements. Their antagonism with the managements, sometimes, amounts to dispute between them. They lead, at times of labour problems, their union members to organise strike in order to get their demands fulfilled. But the response of their union workers is not to a notable extent.

It is, therefore, clear that even the leaders of the Communist unions in both the mills are unable to promote class consciousness among their union workers. This is so due to the neglect and suppression by the managements. That is the reason why a considerable number of members in the Communist unions either leave the unions or have membership in the powerful unions for their job security.

Thus the management policy of favouring the powerful unions and ignoring the powerless unions is an important reason for the disunity of workers. This discrimination makes, undoubtedly, the powerless unions rivals to the powerful unions. This policy of the managements is, therefore, a successful divider of the unions into two hostile camps. This results in inter-union conflict, an inevitable force.

Sometimes, the managements instigate the leaders of the powerful unions to oppose the efforts of their counterparts in powerless unions for personal gains. This is also an important reason for inter-union conflict. This conflict results in widening the gap between the two groups of unions. Thus the union leaders who are expected to be the promoters of class consciousness, do not provide a favourable situation to the workers to get themselves united for class action.

It is observed that the Communist unions in the two mills oppose certain decisions taken by the respective managements regarding the workers' problem. But the managements do not recognize these unions and even go to the extent of suppressing them in different situations. However, the management of mill A does not suppress the Communist unions in all occasions, but ignores them. Generally, their demands are turned down by the management. This results in lack of interest of the members in the union. So a considerable per cent of the members of the AITUC and the CITU in the mills have become members in the powerful unions too. If they have problems, they approach the leaders of the powerful unions for help. The dual membership is found not only among the members of the Communist unions but also among those in other unions including powerful unions.

In spite of these problems, some of the members in the Communist unions retain their membership probably because they are attracted by the power of the propaganda that the party opposes all kinds of oppression by the management. Even the later realization of the ineffectivencess of these unions as compared to others, perhaps, does not wean away the initial enthusiasm and expectations of the members.

A few members of the AITUC and the CITU cancelled their membership and joined the powerful unions to protect their job against victimization. For instance, a former leader of the AITUC was threatened by the then management of mill B that he would lose his promotion if he continues to be the leader of the union. Incidentally he was also served a memo. At last, the helpless leader resigned his post and also cancelled his membership in the union. After that, he was promoted to the maistry's post. Later he joined the HMS, one of the powerful unions recognized by the management.

Though the response of this leader to management shows his vested interest, it is relevant here to see the management's attitude that forced him to be so. Thus the suppression of the Communist unions by the management either drives their members out or make them follow dual membership policy. This is one of the strategies followed by the management of mill B to suppress the emergence of class awareness among the member of the Communist unions.

On the other hand, it is rather difficult to think of the class awareness among the members of the non-Communist unions in both the mills. However, caste loyalties, intra-union conflicts arising out of the power struggle between two dominant castes and inter-union conflicts caused by caste rivalry and instigation of the management are the factors responsible for the absence of class awareness among those members. The succeeding discussions of this chapter also provides some evidence to substantiate this finding.

Workers have many reasons for joining a union. Prakash Arya in his study used nine alternative reasons. The respondents from two plants were asked to choose three of them in the order of importance. The reason which ranked first was "to get a rise in wages".[12] Vaid arrives at a similar conclusion.[13] But Santosh finds that in all the unions a majority of workers say that they joined the union for gaining job security, economic benefits and a better standard of living.[14] In the present study, the respondents gave the reasons as in Table 30.

A majority of the respondents (52.04 per cent) in mill A joined the unions mainly for job security. But more or less a majority of the respondents (49.66 per cent) in mill B joined the union as they wanted their working conditions to be improved through the union. In this mill, five respondents did not join any union as their opinion is that the unions in general do not work for the welfare of the labourers. In the same mill, the respondents who joined the unions to get the workers' demands fulfilled are nearly twice as many as those in mill A. This shows that the idea that the unions

12. P. Prakash Arya, "Workers' Involvement in Trade Unions," *The Indian Journal of Labour Economics* 23 (October 1980): 115-131.
13. K.N. Vaid, "Why Workers join Union ?" *I. dian Journal of Industrial Relations* 1 (October 1965): 208-230
14. Santosh Sood, *Trde Union Leadership in India: A Case Study* (New Delhi: Deep and Deep Publications, 1984), pp. 164-169.

Table 30

Respondents by Reasons for joining the Union/Association

Reasons	*Mill A*	*Mill B*	*Total*
Job security	51 (52.04)	26 (17.11)	77 (30.80)
Standard working conditions	29 (29.59)	73 (48.02)	102 (40.80)
Achieving the demands of workers/staff	18 (18.37)	48 (31.58)	66 (26.40)
Non-members	—	5 (3.29)	5 (2.00)
Total	98 (100.00)	152 (100.00)	250 (100.00)

are formed to fulfil the demands of the workers through certain devices such as representation, collective bargaining and strikes is more realized by the respondents in mill B than by those in mill A.

The history of the unions in the mills explains this phenomenon. It the 1930s, in mill B. the workers from the Naidu caste became members of the Madura Labour Union organized by a Naidu. In other words, unionization among the Naidus was the first instance in the union history of mill B. Afterwards, the workers from the Mukkulathors and the Pillai castes joined other unions formed after the Madura Labour Union. But the unionization among the workers in mill A started only after 1965. Thus the workers in mill B have gained more experience than those in mill A with regard to the various aspects of trade union activity. As regards the respondents from staff, all of them say that they have joined the staff association to achieve their demands.

However, respondents have varied reasons for joining any particular union. Ramaswamy, in one of his studies, points out that the choice of union by respondents depends on work mates, pressure from residential area and numerical superiority of unions.[15] But, in another study, mentions that unionization has not run along caste lines. In other words, caste loyalties have not prevented the workers from enrolling as union members.[16] However, the reasons given by the respondents in the present study differ from this.

As Table 31 shows, more or less a majority of the respondents in both the mills (68.37 per cent in mill A and 48.98 per cent in mill B) have joined unions out of their sympathy with the political parties these unions represent. This trend is reflected in each caste grouping in both the mills. Nearly one-fourth of the respondents in mill B joined the unions considering their comparative strength among the unions. Therefore, there is significant relationship between reasons given by the respondents and their rural-urban background. With regard to the respondents from staff, all of them say that they have joined the particular association mainly for their welfare.

It is evident from the Table that there is relationship between the political involvement of the workers and their inclination to union participation. Sheth who supports this says that the higher the political consciousness of a worker the greater his favourable attitude towards unions.[17] It is found that the degree of political involvement of the respondents is not similar. Consequently, there is a variation in their degree of union participation too.

The level of political involvement—low, medium and high—is obtainned by introducing the following indicators:

(i) attending party meetings,

(ii) meeting local party leaders,

(iii) canvassing and

15. E.A. Ramaswamy, *The Worker and his Union: A Study in South India* (Bombay: Allied, 1977), pp. 47-51.

16. Idem, "Trade Unionism and Caste in South India," *Modern Asian Students* 10 (1976): 361-373.

17. N.R. Sheth and S.P. Jain, "Workers, leaders, and politics," *Indian Journal of Industrial Relations* 3 (January 1978): 286-289.

Table 31

Castes of the Respondents by their Reasons for joining any particular Union/Association

Reasons	*Mukkulathor*		*Pillai*		*Naidu*		*Harijan*		*Other Castes*		*Total*	
	A	*B*	*A*	*B*	*A*	*B*	*A*	*B*	*A*	*B*	*A*	*B*
Out of interest in party affiliation	16	28	14	8	4	15	14	5	19	16	67 (68.37)	72 (48.98)
Caste affinity	3	8	1	4	1	3	1	1	2	4	8 (8.16)	20 (13.61)
Power of the union	4	15	1	4	1	3	2	3	5	11	13 (13.27)	36 (24.49)
Fulfilling the workers' needs	2	7	1	4	1	3	2	1	4	4	10 (10.20)	19 (12.92)
Total	25	58	17	20	7	24	19	10	30	35	98 (100.00)	147 (100.00)

Note: A and B refer to mill A and mill B respectively. In mill B, N=147 in this Table because five respondents are non-members.

$X^2=9.491$ df=3 $P<0.05$

(iv) participating in programmes organized by party organization (in Tamil known as "Mandram"). The four-item index "political involvement" gives score types, one to eight. The scores for the items are given below:

Item	*All*	*A Few*	*None*
(i)	2	1	0
(ii)	2	1	0
(iii)	2	1	0
(iv)	2	1	0

Note: The four itemes listed above are in the same order as that shown in this paragraph.

The scores are grouped into three categories: low (scores 1, 2, 3); medium (scores 4, 5); and high (scores 6, 7, 8).

The union participation of the respondents—low, medium and high—is arrived at by a similar procedure. The criteria are:

(i) attending union meeting,
(ii) participating in discussions during union meeting,
(iii) canvassing at the time of union election, and
(iv) supporting strikes organised by the union. The four-item index "union participation" gives score types, one to eight. The scores for the items are given below:

Item	*All*	*A Few*	*None*
(i)	2	1	0
(ii)	2	1	0
(iii)	2	1	0
(iv)	2	1	0

Note: The four items listed above are in the same order as that shown in this paragraph.

The scores are grouped into three categories: low (scores 1, 2, 3); medium (scores 4, 5) and high (scores 6, 7, 8).

Before considering the relationship between union participation and political involvement, it is important to study these two aspects separately. The level of union/association participation of the respondents in mill A and mill B differ from caste to caste.

On the whole the percentage of respondents, whose level of participation is low, is more or less the same as the percentage of those whose level of participation is high. A high percentage of respondents (about one-half) from castes such as the Mukkulathor and the Pillai show high level of union participation, whereas only limited respondents (about one-fourth) from castes such as the Naidu and the Harijan show high level of union participation. This can be explained by the fact that the first two dominant castes—the Mukkulathor and the Pillai—in terms of numerical strength participate in the unions at the high level. Though the Harijans occupy the second place with regard to numerical strength, a fairly high percentage of them show low union participation because of their inhibitions which continue to endure. The low level participation of the Naidus may be explained in terms of their low numerical strength. More or less a similar trend is found in mill B.

On the whole the percentage of respondents whose level of participation is high is fairly high (42.86 per cent) in the mill. A majority of the respondents from Mukkulathor caste show a high level union participation as a clear contrast to the other castes such as the Pillai, the Naidu and the Harijan. Especially a majority of Harijans show a low level union participation The percentages of the Naidus (42.31) and the Pillais (38.10) showing high level participation are more or less similar. The reason may be that the numerical strength of Mukkulathors outnumbers the other castes. The Harijans who are at the other extreme in numerical strength show the largest percentage of low level participation among the four castes.

Table 32

Union/Association Participation of the Respondents in Mill A by their Castes

Union/ Association Participation	*Mukkulathor*	*Pillai*	*Naidu*	*Harijan*	*Other Castes*	*Total*
Low	7 (28.00)	6 (35.29)	3 (42.86)	9 (47.37)	9 (30.00)	34 (34.69)
Medium	2 (8.00)	4 (23.53)	2 (28.57)	6 (31.58)	13 (43.33)	27 (27.55)
High	16 (64.00)	7 (41. 8)	2 (28.57)	4 (21.05)	8 (26.67)	37 (37.76)
Total	25 (100.00)	17 (100.00)	7 (100.00)	19 (100.00)	30 (100.00)	98 (100.00)

$X^2=17.023$ df=8 $P<0.05$

Table 33

Union/Association Participation of the Respondents in Mill B by their Castes

Union/ Association Participation	*Mukkulathor*	*Pillai*	*Naidu*	*Harijan*	*Other Castes*	*Total*
Low	10 (18.18)	6 (28.57)	8 (30.77)	5 (50.00)	16 (45.71)	45 (30.61)
Medium	11 (20.00)	7 (33.33)	7 (26.92)	2 (20.00)	12 (34 92)	39 (26.53)
High	34 (61.82)	8 (38.10)	11 (42 31)	3 (30.00)	7 (20.00)	63 (42.86)
Total	55 (100.00)	21 (100.00)	26 (100.00)	10 (100.00)	35 (100.00)	147 (100 00)

$X^2 = 17.426$ df=8 $P < 0.05$

From Tables 32 and 33, it is found that there is significant relationship between the union participation of the respondents and numerical strength of their castes. But for the purpose of the analysis only four castes (the Mukkulathors, the Pillai, the Naidu and the Harijan) are taken into consideration. The participation of the "other castes" in union activities is not included in the analysis of the Tables because of their meagre number individually. However, it is evident from these Tables that the difference between the ural and urban respondents with regard to their union participation is not considerably distinct. It is inferred from this that the rural-urban background of the respondents has no impact on their union participation.

Table 34

Union/Association Participation of the Respondents by their Rural-Urban Backgrounds

Union/Association Participation	*Mill A*	*Mill B*	*Total*
Low	34 (34.69)	45 (30.6)	79 (32.24)
Medium	27 (27.55)	39 (26.53)	66 (26.94)
High	37 (37.76)	63 (42.86)	100 (40.82)
Total	98 (100.00)	147 (100 00)	245 (100.00)

$X^2=0.648$ df=2 $P>0.05$

As regards union participation at high level, the percentage of respondents (42.86) in mill B is slightly higher than that of those (37.76) in mill A. Similarly the difference in percentages of the respondents with regard to medium and low level union participation is marginal. Therefore, there is no significant relationship between union participation of the respondents and their rural-urban backgrounds. This finding is in agreement with that of Sharma who shows that the rural-urban background of his sample workers does not seem to influence their union participation.[18]

It is relevant here to find out whether there is relationship between the level of political involvement of the respondents and their castes.

The castes such as the Mukkulathor, the Pillai, the Naidu and the Harijan occupy first, second, third and fourth places respectively with regard to political involvement. The difference among the first four castes with regard to the high level of their political involvement is significant. Hence the significant relationship between the level of political involvement of the respondents and their castes. A similar trend is fʈ und in mill B.

With regard to the level of political involvemnt, the Mukkulathors occupy the first place; the Pillais and the Naidus occupy the second and third places respectively leaving the fourth place to the Harijans. The difference among the first four castes is considerable as found in mill A with regard to their high level political involvement. So it is proved that there is significant relationship between the level of political involvement of the respondents and their castes.

It is inferred from the Tables 35 and 36 that the rural-urban background of the respondents has its impact on their political involvement.

On the whole the percentage of respondents with high political involvement is not very much (42.86 per cent). But more respondents in mill B (48.98 per cent) have higher political involvement than those (33.67 per cent) in mill A. It is also proved that there is significant relationship between the level of political involvement of the respondents and their rural-urban backgrounds. In other words, the urban workers show more involvement in politics than the rural workers. In urban centres like Madurai, the workforce and other population are exposed to the day-to-day developments in politics.

18. Baldev Raj Sharma, *The Industrial Workers: Issues in Perspective* (Delhi: Vikas, 1974), p. 121.

Table 35

Political Involvement of the Respondents in Mill A by their Castes

Political involvement	*Mukkulathor*	*Pillai*	*Naidu*	*Harijan*	*Other castes*	*Total*
Low	6	5	3	11	18	43
	(24.00)	(29.41)	(42.86)	(57.89)	(60.00)	(43.88)
Medium	4	3	1	6	8	22
	(16.00)	(17.65)	(14.28)	(31.58)	(26.67)	(22.55)
High	15	9	3	2	4	33
	(60.00)	(52.94)	(42.86)	(10.53)	(13.33)	(33.67)
Total	25	17	7	19	30	98
	(100.00)	(100.00)	(100.00)	(100.00)	(100.00)	(100.00)

$X^2 = 23.748$ $\quad$ $df = 8$ $\quad$ $P < 0.05$

Table 36

Political Involvement of the Respondents in Mill B by their Castes

Political involvement	*Mukkulathor*	*Pillai*	*Naidu*	*Harijan*	*Other castes*	*Total*
Low	11 (20.00)	5 (23.81)	8 (32.81)	5 (50.00)	11 (30.55)	40 (27.21)
Medium	9 (16.36)	4 (19.05)	5 (20.00)	2 (20.00)	15 (41.67)	35 (23.81)
High	35 (63.64)	12 (57.14)	12 (48.00)	3 (20.00)	10 (27.78)	72 (48.98)
Total	55 (100.00)	21 (100.00)	25 (100.00)	10 (100.00)	36 (100.00)	147 (100.00)

$X^2=15.878$ df=8 $P<0.05$

Table 37

Political Involvement of the Respondents by their Rural-Urban Background

Political involvement	*Mill A*	*Mill B*	*Total*
Low	43 (43.88)	40 (27.21)	83 (33.88)
Medium	22 (22.45)	35 (23.81)	57 (23.26)
High	33 (33.67)	72 (48.98)	105 (42.86)
Total	98 (100.00)	147 (100.00)	245 (100 00)

$X^2=8.317$ df=2 $P<0.05$

They have a number of chances to attend political meetings addressed by high level leaders of political parties. They have party associations (named after the founder of their party). They conduct a number of meetings, processions and agitations on instructions from the high level leaders of their parties. These advantages are not enjoyed by their counterparts in rural areas. This may be the reason why there are more respondents with high level of political involvement in the urban mill than in the rural mill.

However, it is relevant here to find out whether there is relationship between political involvement of the respondents and their union participation.

In mill A, the union participation of the respondents depends on their political involvement. In other words, the higher the political involvement of the respondents, the higher their union participation. It is thus evident that there is high significant relationship between the union participation of the respondents and their political involvement.

Similarly, there is significant relationship between the union participation of the respondents and their political involvement in mill B.

Table 38

Relationship between Union Participation of the Respondents and their Political Involvement in Mill A

Union Participation	*Political involvement*			*Total*
	Low	*Medium*	*High*	
Low	23 (53.49)	6 (27.28)	5 (15.15)	34 (34.69)
Medium	11 (25.58)	8 (36.36)	8 (24.24)	27 (27.55)
High	9 (20.93)	8 (36.36)	20 (60.61)	37 (37.76)
Total	43 (100.00)	22 (100.00)	33 (100.00)	98 (100.00)

$X^2=15.733$ df=4 $P<0.05$

In mill B also, the union participation of the respondents depends on their political involvement. In other words, the higher their political involvement, the higher their union participation. It is proved that there is very high significant relationship between the union participation of the respondents and their political involvement.

All the sample staff in both mills show a low level participation in their associations. The reason for this is explained later. Similarly most of them (four out of six in mill A and seven out of eleven in mill B) show a low level political involvement.

In both the mills, a few respondents (20.93 per cent in mill A and ten per cent in mill B), irrespective of their low level of political involvement, show a high level of union participation. This can be explained in terms of the caste loyalty of the respondents towards their union leaders. For instance, if a member belongs to the caste of his leader, he would support him irrespective of other differences. In case his leader commits an error he does not want to complain against him. This does not indeed mean that all the

Table 39

Relationship between Union Participation of the Resondents and their Political Iuvolvement in Mill B

Union Participation	*Political Involvement*			
	Low	*Medium*	*High*	*Total*
Low	4 (10.00)	5 (14.28)	36 (50.00)	45 (30.61)
Medium	13 (32.50)	11 (31.43)	15 (20.83)	39 (26 53)
High	23 (57.50)	19 (54.29)	21 (29.17)	63 (42.86)
Total	40 (100.00)	35 (100.00)	72 (100.00)	147 (100.00)

$X^2=25.576$ df=4 $P<0.05$

respondents belonging to the caste of their leader would follow this principle.

In mill A, of 24 respondents who belong to the caste of their union leaders, only five (20.83 per cent) complain against them as against nineteen (79.17 per cent) who do not complain. So the readiness to complain against leaders on the part of the respondents depends upon the castes of these two categories. In other words, the respondents avoid complaining against their union leaders if the leaders belong to their caste. In case the leaders belong to other castes, the respondents develop a prejudice against their leaders. But this trend is different in mill B. A considerable percentage (39.02) of the respondents of this mill, though belong to the caste of their union leaders, complain against them. Normally their complaints are of corruption, caste loyalty and vested interest. The statistical test shows that there is significant relationship between castes of the respondents from mill A and mill B and their complaints against the union leaders.

Table 40

Respondents by their Complaints against their Leaders

Caste of the respondents	*Complain sgainst leaders* *Mill A* *Yes*	*No*	*Mill B* *Yes*	*No*	*Total* *Mill A*	*Mill B*
Belonging to the caste of leaders	5 (20.83)	19 (79.17)	32 (39.02)	50 (60.98)	24 (100.00)	82 (100.00)
Belonging to other castes	44 (59.46)	30 (40.54)	38 (58.46)	27 (41.54)	74 (100.00)	65 (100.00)
Total	49 (50.00)	49 (50.00)	70 (47.62)	77 (52.38)	98 (100.00)	147 (100.00)

Mill A : $X^2=10.814$ df=1 $P<0.05$

Mill B : $X^2=5.418$ df=1 $P \lessdot 0.05$

However, the significance in the relationship is higher in mill A than in mill B. This indicates that caste affinity among the workers is more in the rural mill than in the urban mill.

All the sample staff in the mills do not complain against the leaders of their associations, but they say that their leaders are ineffective. They continue to be the leaders for name sake.

An attempt is made to find out whether the leaders favour their castemen in their unions. The opinions of the respondents were obtained on this question. It is found that the union leaders help their castemen with regard to solving their problems arising out of absenteeism, work load, promotion and partiality of maistrys and the factory staff.

In mill A, the respondents who say that their union leaders favour their castemen are more or less twice as many as those in mill B. But in mill B, the respondents who say that their leaders favour those providing monetary and non-monetary help on the one hand and those applicable to both categories on the other hand are about twice as many as those in mill A. In both the mills, the respondents whose opinions are neutural and those who have no idea on the subject constitute more or less a similar percentage. However, it is proved that there is significant relationship between the rural-urban background of the respondents and their opinions regarding favouritism of their union leaders. But all the respondents from the staff say that their association leaders are neutral in dealing with the problems of the members.

Generally, the respondents do not like the favouritism of the leaders either to their castemen or to those who extend their help to them. In both the mills, an overwhelming majority of the respondents (90.22 per cent in mill A and 97.06 per cent in mill B) say that this would weaken the solidarity of the union.

Similarly, thc respondents do not like the involvement of caste relations in the union. A large majority of the respondents (94.57 per cent in mill A and 98.53 per cent in mill B) belong to this category. This is because of the reason given by them that the involvement of caste relations in unions would weaken their strength and unity. This observation

Table 41

Background of the Respondents and their Opinions regarding the Favouritism of their Leaders

Mill	*Favourable to castemen*	*Favourable to those who extend their help*	*Both*	*Neutral*	*No idea*	*Total*
A	24 (24.49)	11 (11.22)	5 (5.80)	46 (46.94)	12 (12.25)	98 (100.00)
B	22 (14.97)	26 (17.69)	19 (12.92)	63 (42.86)	17 (11.56)	147 (100.00)
Total	46 (18.78)	37 (15.10)	24 (9.79)	109 (44.49)	29 (11.84)	245 (100.00)

$X^2 = 9.666$ df=4 $P < 0.05$

shows the discrepancy between what the respondents believe and what they practise.

It is important here to discuss the monetary and non-monetary help the workers give their union leaders. Generally the leaders expect money from the members of the union to attend to their problems. A few of the respondents (one from mill A and six from mill B) report that had they bribed their union leaders, they would have become maistrys much earlier. Again a few respondents (three from mill B) say that had they bribed their union leaders, they would have been transferred to other departments for lighter work. Of the seven union secretaries in mill B, two acknowledge that they received money from a few workers to recommend their candidates to the management for recruitment as workers.

Even when the problems of the workers are genuine and have the sympathy of others, they expect money from them to attend them. A senior maistry in mill B explains the tragic end of his son caused by the negligence of his union leader:

> In 1980, with great difficulty I introduced my son in the mill as a worker. There was a rule that a worker's wages should be fixed after the completion of six months as a trainee. But my son's wages were not fixed after the stipulated period. I approached my union leader to represent this to the management. He agreed to help with the expectation that I would give him a sizable amount of money. His plan was to take up the issue only after receiving the money. Since he belonged to my caste, I did not think that he had such an expectation. After a few days I understood that he was a bit casual in this matter. In spite of my repeated requests he did not take any step. Somehow I came to know that he expected money from me. As my family was large, I was unable to bribe him. I was not even able to give my son some pocket money. One day he committed suicide as he lost the hope of getting his wages. If the leader had helped in this matter, my son would have been alive now.

A worker in mill B is very much annoyed with the union leaders for their vested interests.

> Union leaders are directed by personal motives. They enjoy benefits at the cost of the workers. For instance in 1973 the workers wanted to organize a strike against increased work load. Before 1973, a worker in the spinning section had to produce 500 spindles in his shift. But in 1973, they were asked to produce 600 spindles within the specified time. They refused to do so because from their point of view, the work load was heavy. The leaders of the dominant unions (the PTMK, the INTUC and the HMS) decided to support the new load policy with an intention to derive some benefit from the management. So they appealed to the workers to co-operate with the management. But the workers refused to agree to the revised work load. They lost faith in their leaders as they thought that the leaders wanted to safeguard the interests of the management. They criticised their leader in such circumstance, the other unions (such as the MTC, the AITUC, and the CITU) came forward to extend their co-operation to the workers. As a result, most of the workers in the INTUC, the PTMK and the HMS unions cancelled their membership. They formed an adhoc union with the name "The Meenakshi Mills United Labour Union" mainly to organize a strike against the new work load. The minority unions joined the new union to get their demand fulfilled. The strike went on for 95 days. However, it was a failure. If the leaders of the dominant unions had supported the strike, the management would have withdrawn the new policy on work load.

A similar incident in mill A shows the vested interest of the union leaders. Before 1980, the workers in each shift were given the provision of rest time for thirty minutes. The production in all the departments was stopped during this time. But, in 1980 the SIMA (South India Mills' Association) announced that stopping the production for thirty minutes was unscientific because it was a loss to the management. It suggested that the workers dividing themselves into two groups could avail this facility by turns. In other words, when the first group in each department rests, the second group attends to the work of the first group along with their work. The same procedure has to be followed by the first group when the second group rests.

The management of mill A wanted to implement this plan in 1980. The leaders of the Communist unions strongly opposed it, whereas the leaders of the non-Communist unions supported it. This resulted in verbal conflict between the workers of the Communist unions and those of the non-Communist unions. It is said that a considerable number of workers in the non-Communist unions did not like that plan. However, their leaders decided to continue their support to the management with an intention to get certain benefits. The Management also wanted their support to implement the plan.

Since the workers of the Communist unions were very vigorus in opposing it, the verbal conflict between them and their opponents led to physical assault. The conflict ended after the immediate arrival of police force. A few workers from both sides were arrested. At last the management implemented the plan after the approval of the leaders of the majority unions. The role of the leaders of the powerful unions in this is highly notable.

After sometime, these leaders were promoted as oilers. This made it clear to the workers of the Communist unions that the leaders supported the management mainly for their promotions. From their point of view, the leaders had gained personal benefits at the cost of the workers. A few members of the non-Communist unions felt so, too. Such incidents in both the mills show that the union leaders are interested in personal gains.

Another incident of this sort in mill B shows the vested interest of the leaders of the powerful unions. In 1986, the union leaders together organised a strike to press the management to increase their wage. For the first four days all the union leaders were united in their effort. On the fifth day the

INTUC, the HMS and the ATS leaders suggested to the other union leaders that they might withdraw the strike because the former were influenced by the management indirectly to break the strike. But the other union leaders did not want to do so. The powerful union leaders with an expectation to get certain benefits from the management asked their union members to resume their work.

The management was happy about the decision taken by the leaders of the powerful unions, but dissatisfied with the other unions which continued the strike. The leaders and members of these unions criticized the powerful unions for their indifferent attitude. Those who entered the mill were provided with food and shelter so that they could avoid physical assault by the aggrisved workers who were outside the mill. The workers who were inside the mill attended their work by enjoying the facilities provided by the management. After ten days, the helpless workers who were outside the mill, resumed work with discontentment. Thus the strike ended in total failure. That is the reason why a majority of the respondents in both the mills say that their leaders are interested in personal gains.

Table 42
Respondents' Views on their Leaders by their Rural-Urban Backgronnd

Respondents' View	*Mill A*	*Mill B*
Interested in personal gains	64 (65.31)	88 (59 86)
Interested in union welfare	14 (14.29)	19 (12.93)
Intarested in personal gains and welfare of their castemen	12 (12.24)	24 (16.33)
No idea	8 (8.16)	16 (10.88)
Total	98 (100.00)	147 (100.00)

$x^2 = 1.528$ df = 3 $P>0.05$

Note : Since the staff associations in the mills are ineffective, all the respondents from the staff uniformly mention that they have nothing to say about their leaders.

In both the mills, a majority of the respondents (65.31, per cent in mill A and 59.86 per cent in mill B) say that their union leaders are interested in their personal gains. Almost all the sample workers from the Communist unions (five out of six in mill A and all the nine in mill B) express that their leaders are interested in union welfare. Since the difference in the views of the respondents in both the mills regarding their leaders is not distinct, there is no significant relationship between their views and their rural-urban backgrounds. This is supported by the finding of Mamkoottam that a majority of union members (64.64 per cent) feel that the Tata workers' union leaders are interested in their personal gains.[19]

Sheth refers to one of his respondents' view which also supports this finding of the present study.

> The leaders are no leaders at all. They work for their own stomach and families as we do. When we seek their help they often say they have no time to attend to us. They attend conferences and meetings with the money we subscribe. They boast they represent our interest in conferences etc., but actually they go to enjoy themselves in cities···our money is merely wasted.[20]

The union leaders who have vested interests, are also corrupt to a certain extent. This is corroborated by the information collected from the Labour Welfare Officer in mill A. He says that if a worker approaches a leader for help, the leader would not discuss the problem him with or the Managing Director. He would take the issue to the conciliation office at Madurai since he wants to enjoy the provision of "on duty" leave. Most of the leaders do so irrespective of the nature of the problem. The concerned worker has to attend to the needs

19. K. Mamkoottam, "Factionalism and Power in Trade Unions: Case Study," *Indian Journal of Industrial Relations* 13 (October 1977): 167-190.
20. N.R. Sheth, "Trade Union in an India Factory: A Sociological Analysis," *The Economic Weekly* 12 (July 1960): 1159-1161.

of the leader for the whole day. Sometime, the leader would demand a sizeable amount to solve his problem. This was a regular practice of the leaders for three years. The reason was that the then Managing Director was liberal in dealing with the leaders because he did not want to face the problems arising out of their demands. Hence the leaders mostly avoid discussing problems with the Labour Welfare Officer or the Managing Director. But this was checked by the successive Managing Directors.

The vested interests and corruption of the union leaders are mainly responsible for the dissatisfaction of the members with their unions. A fairly high percentage of the union members (40 per cent in mill A and 42 per cent in mill B) are not satisfied with the activities of their unions. This tendency would not promote the class-consciousness among the members.

It is evident from the discussion that like the management, the corruption and vested interests of the union leaders on the one hand and the caste loyalty of the union leaders as well as the workers on the other, prevent the emergence of class consciousness among the workers. The class consciousness is dependent variable, whereas the management, union leadership and caste loyalty are independent variables. But the corruption and vested interests of the union leaders are influenced by the other two variables. In otherwords, the vested interests of the union leaders are encouraged by the caste loyalty. Similarly, the corruption of the union leaders is promoted by the favourable attitude of the management. Figure 3 shows the relationship of these variables with one another.

As regards the staff in both the mills, the disunity among them results in the absence of class awareness as "middle management". This trend was observed by the investigator in various interacting situations. In mill A, the staff—technical and non-technical—constitute 61 members. They have three different staff associations. The technical staff organised two separate associations. But there is only one association formed by 110 staff of mill B.

FIGURE 3

Variables Affecting Class Consciousness of the Workers in the Mills

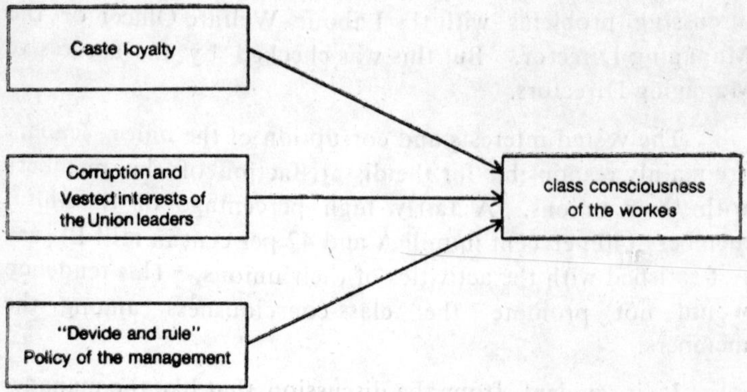

These associations were formed with a view to promote the welfare of the staff through their organised efforts in terms of representing their legitimate demands to the management. But it is observed that they are neither active nor effective in their functions. In other words, lack of interest of members in their association results in ineffectiveness of the associations. In addition to this, the associations are financially instable and politically weak.

Generally, the staff do not want to represent either their grievances or demands through their associations. Individually they meet the management for their problems. Therefore, it is a question of individual effort on the part of the staff to redress their grievances. They also approach the management with regard to matters such as conducting cultural programmes, seeking permission for few hours to attend the marriage of any staff or death in any staff's family. The limited functions of the associations do not attract the staff to aspire for leadership position. This is the reason why there is no competition among them for leadership position.

In mill A (a co-operative sector), it is observed that the staff in general are content with regard to the treatment of the management. Since the management adhere to the rules stipulated by the Government, everything goes as it is expected to be. There are rare incidents of anomaly regarding staff selection or their promotion, but it would be checked and rectified in the course of time by the successive Managing Directors. The staff feel that they would not be affected by the change of Managing Directors because they are invariably the government employees, that is, IAS officers.

But, in mill B (a private sectoa), most of the staff are dissatisfied with the present management. They have experienced two different managements within a period of three years besides their long experience with the Nagarathar management. During the time of the Nagarathar management, the staff in general did not feel discomfort because of their fair treatment. Similarly, during the management of Central Bank of India, they enjoyed more or less the same provisions as extended to them by the previous management. They felt free to approach the management for their problems. Most of them have full appreciation to the management for their fair dealings with the staff in certain matters. But now they feel discomfort because of the reshuffling made by Dalmia group at the top and the middle management. They also feel that the Dalmia management has exercised their power even to the extent of suppressing a few senior officials by appointing their kinsmen in certain key posts. They have also appointed a few known persons who are loyal to them at the middle management level to deal with vital issues of the workers. Certain facilities enjoyed by the staff have been stopped suddenly. The staff are instructed to complete the work assigned to them in a day irrespective of usual working hours prescribed to them.

In spite of all these, the staff association remains inactive as its members do not have the courage to meet the management for their grievances. They have a feeling that they would be troubled if they represent their dmands through their association. In November, 1986, they experienced a bitter event which is summarised by one of the staff as follows:

> The workers of the mill organised a strike in November, 1986 for certain demands. The main demand was that the workers who had completed three years of regular training period have to be given category wages and made permanent. A few days after the commencement of the strike, the staff were prevented by the workers from entering the mill in order to get their support. As a result, the staff issued a strike notice to the management in support of the workers. This was mainly because of the reason that the staff also wanted to fulfil certain demand in this crucial circumstance. As proposed, the leaders and a few members in the staff association met the management with the expectation that their demands would also be considered favourably along with the demands of the workers.
>
> However, the members of staff association did not have similar view regarding this issue. A few of them directly opposed it because of the fear that all the staff would be troubled by the management in the course of time. A considerable number of them remained silent spectators. Even the leaders of the association met the management with some trepidation. As feared by them, the management expressed their displeasure over this representation. They gave vent to their feelings of anger and annoyance by sarcastically remarking that the staff may also join the workers to protest against the management for their demands. They withheld the salary of staff from payment during the strike period. A group of staff who were loyal to the management had been feeding them information frequently regarding the agitating staff and the trend of the strike. After a couple of weeks, the staff association withdrew their strike notice and extended its co-operation to the management with the expectation that their demands would be achieved through negotiation. But few staff did not like this.

This led to a split in the staff association resulting in disunity.

It seems that the inactiveness of the members of staff association is due to their lack of interest and the fear of confronting the management at times of their demands. However, these reasons are apparent. What is true is that, like the labour union, the staff association has also become the target of the management to get it either divided or dissolved. That is how the unity of staff is deliberately prevented. As a result, there is no chance of the emergence of class consciousness among the staff.

The formation of caste groupings among the staff are also hindrance to the development of their class awareness. Such groups are observed among the staff of both the mills. The leaders of staff associations patronize their caste groupings. In mill A, especially, the Pillais, the Naidus and the Mukkulathors form small groups of their castemen to discuss their personal matters and other problems, during lunch break. They indulge in carping criticism of the staff from other castes. Similar groups are observed in mill B. Especially, the staff from the Sourashtra and the Nagarathar castes have such groupings. This would normally restrict their movements with the staff from other castes. They do not easily get rid of caste loyalties which also prevent the emergence of class consciousness among the staff.

Figure 4 shows the impact of the independent variables—lack of interest of the staff in their association, fear of confronting the management at times of problems and 'divide and rule' policy of the management—on the staff associations in terms of preventing the class consciousness among the staff.

To conclude, in the non-Communist unions, the castes consisting of a majority or fairly high percentage of members bring their men to power. Thus union loyalty is replaced by caste loyalty. Intra-union conflicts arising out of the power struggle between two dominant castes, inter-union conflicts caused by caste rivalry and the vested interests of the union leaders and the instigation of the management are the major

FIGURE 4

Variables Affecting Class Consciousness of the Staff in the Mills

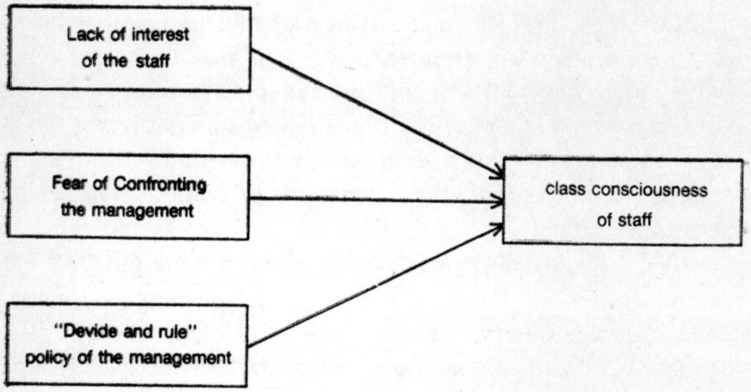

factors preventing the class consciousness among the workers from the non-Communist unions.

On the other hand, in the Communist unions, the non-commitment of the workers either to their unions or to their parties, feeling of insecurity and negligence and sometimes suppression of their unions by the management are the main reasons for the absence of class consciousness among them.

As regards staff associations in both the mills, they are mostly inactive. The disunity among the staff results in the absence of class consciousness as "middle management". This disunity may be the result of caste loyalty of the staff and their lack of interest in their associations. The lack of interest may also be due to the absence of financial stability and political support in their associations. Moreover, the fear of the staff that they would be victimized if they actively involve in their association activities, is also responsible for their disunity. But in mill B, the instigation of the management is also an important reason for the disunity of the staff association.

7

Conclusion

Industrialization in India has provided scope for upward mobility for the low castes. In other words, it has narrowed down the yawning gap between the high and the low castes. This study has attempted to find out how far an industry has reduced the functions of caste and prepared the ground for the emergence of class among its employees.

The idea that class distinctions emerge as a result of changes taking place in caste system is supported by some scholars like Beteille, Anil Bhatt and D'Souza. But other scholars such as Hutton, Furnivall and Oscar Lewis mention that caste is stable and at times it even reinforces itself. But neither of these contentions is fully true of contemporary India. Though caste has not found full expression in the industrial scene, it has not disappeared or even substantially weakened. It continues to exist in India assuming new functions in accordance with changing social situations. It has proved its resilience, its capacity to adopt itself to new challenging situations, and to preserve its core in this complex society.

But the emergence of a "working class" as a category in industrial cities of contemporary India is evident. This gives rise to a new situation in which caste and class co-exist.

Classes have not crystallised yet in India. So this attempt has been made to study the caste and class relations in two spinning mills situated in Madurai District, which are of contrasting nature with regard to size, age, location and ownership.

Generally industry does not provide scope for the formation of caste-based relationship among its population. But the workers in rural mill have membership in their caste associations formed within the mill. A few such associations have sizeable (45 per cent to 60 per cent) members from the majority castes. Workers from a few minority castes are members of their caste associations formed outside the mill. Though such associations are not found within the mill situated in the urban area, an average of 27 per cent of the workers from certain castes are members in their respective caste associations formed outside the mill.

All those who are members in caste associations are also members in trade unions. The main purpose of the union is to unite workers irrespective of caste differences for a common cause. It is expected to promote class consciousness among the workers in order to make them aware of their position in relation to the capitalists and their rights as workers. But the very purpose of the union has not been fulfilled because of the caste loyalties of the workers. Such loyalties are strengthened by the caste associations. It is possible that the formation of a few caste associations within the mill will motivate the other castes to form their associations in future. The emergence of class consciousness among the workers is thus very much retarded. Unless they have this class consciousness, they cannot form a "class for itself" in the Marxian point of view.

In this study, education, occupation and income are used to classify the respondents into different class categories. This is mainly because of the reason that the respondents belonging to different educational, occupational and income groups may identify themselves with others from similar groups. Nevertheless, the workers constitute a class apparently. But they do not have class consciousness which is essential for class action. The present study supports this observation with the help of available data.

The pattern of management has its impact on the attitudes of workers and staff. The mill in the rural area falls under the co-operative sector. It is regulated by the Government's rules. So since 1974, recruitment of employees in the mill has been made through the Government's Employment Exchange, maintaining a certain proportion in the representation to Backward and Scheduled Castes. Yet the recruitment policy followed prior to the introduction of the new system, based on the caste to which the mill authorities belonged, has gone on long enough to establish a certain communal pattern that cannot be disturbed easily or early. The same pattern applies to the office staff in the mill.

The results of these developments are clear. The workers establish relationship mostly with men of their caste. They do not have awareness of class solidarity. At the same time, there is no complete awareness of class distinctions, either. However, a majority of the respondents in both the mills do not meet the staff members for their personal problems mainly because of the assumed difference in the status of these two categories of employees. Instead they approach their maistrys and the union leaders for this. But this does not mean that they have the awareness of their position in relation to the staff members. This is more a development of in-group feeling than an indicator of the emergence of class consciousness.

Now, under the government regulated promotion policy, caste is not a determining factor in the rural mill. At least, in the course of time, anomalies in promotions are checked by the successive Managing Directors. That is the reason why nearly two-thirds of the respondents from this mill say that promotions are according to seniority. Some workers and staff members are, however, recommended by union leaders and officials for promotion.

In the urban mill, which is privately owned, recruitment of employees in the early days was greatly influenced by considerations of caste and exigencies. As in the rural mill, the management of the urban mill was responsible for the caste composition of the workforce. The workers especially the maistrys were also partly responsible for this. But in the last ten years the leaders from the powerful unions have played a vital role in recruitment of workers. This system still continues: recruitment depends on the payment of sizeable amount to the union leaders. Irrespective of caste, a worker enters the mill by paying the sum fixed by the union leaders as their personal tribute. The corruption of the leaders has thus disillusioned the workers with their leaders at the very start of their career, and made them rather cynical about the altruistic motives of unionism itself.

The situation has serious consequences for class consciousness among workers. The management protects its interests by giving certain benefits to the leaders of the powerful unions, who claim to be the custodians of working class interests, thus driving a wedge between the leaders and the workers on the one hand and between the majority and the minority unions on the other hand. This naturally results in inter and intra-union conflicts which do not promote the class solidarity.

The staff recruitment is made by the management itself. The Nagarathar management brought in a few men of their own caste but had to recruit a few men from a community that dominates the textile industry in this part of the country for higher posts, and this community managed to enter the office in a fairly high proportion. In recent years, the mill has changed hands. For a short period, a bank managed it. But now the mill is under the control of a North Indian businessman who has introduced a considerable number of his men. Generally, among the staff, there is no unity based on an awareness of their common interests and identity. Thus neither the staff nor the workers have class consciousness.

It is evident that caste is less of guiding force in the urban mill than in the rural mill. This observation may justify the finding of some studies that industrialization is more influential in the urban area in which caste is less evident in its organisation. However, this does not mean that even in urban area caste has disappeared altogether as a guiding force.

Promotions in this mill are a different matter. The influence of union leaders is considerably less in this regard than in the matter of labour recruitment. The influence of maistrys is far more weighty. The maistrys are workers who have come up by dint of experience and service. This means that they belong to the old order where the workers belonging to certain castes were recruited on a large scale. These old hands are still loyal to their castes. Thus their recommendations naturally follow caste line It is also observed by some workers that union leaders also are more attentive to the claims of their own castes in the matter of promotions. So one-third of the respondents in the mill state that the promotion is through the influence of union leaders and maistrys. Thus the vested interests of both the union leaders and the maistrys also cause disunity among the workers and intensify their caste relations.

In interacting situations, the polarization of employees towards caste is more pronounced in rural mill than in the urban mill. Especially the Mukkulathors in both the mills are widely distributed in all the departments. In the rural mill, they interact mostly among themselves. This trend is not so evident in the urban mill. This observation reveals the impact of the social background on interaction. A considerable number of respondents from minority castes in the mills are afraid of the Mukkulathors, especially the Kallars who, according to them, resort to violence even for simple matters when the other party belongs to some other caste. That is, caste as a divisive force is more evident in the rural mill than in the urban mill. This observation is confirmed by the study of workers' choice of friends for certain matters relating to financial and other assistance, counselling and other such affairs.

A few observations of the studies on industries have been proved right by this study. Since the rural and urban mills have brought together men of different castes, the rigidity of caste distinctions has lessened. Indeed they have not lessened so radically as to admit the traditional untouchables (Harijans) into leadership positions. Yet a large majority of the Caste-Hindu respondents move with the Harijans without reservations. All the Harijan respondents in both the mills say that they are not avoided by the Caste-Hindus for pollution. They also acknowledge that that they move with the Caste-Hindus without inhibitions and dine with them in public.

In most non-Communist unions, caste is still a dominant factor. This is especially so in the rural mill. The Communist unions are to some extent an exception to this. But the mill managements seek to minimise their power by keeping them out of discussions concerning labour problems. This has weakened the Communist unions in terms of membership support. The managements promote sectional interests to safeguard their interests. The non-Communist unions have less of a policy orientation and lend themselves much more readily to sectional and divisive forces.

The role of the management in the development of self-conscious labour class is bound to be significant. The management in its own interest likes to eliminate the development of such class awareness. This tendency is very much evident in the private sector mill. It pampers the leaders of the powerful unions and succeeds in slowly alienating them from workforce. It also makes the workforce lose faith in union leaders first and in unionism itself ultimately. Since the Communist unions do not accept the settlements or decisions taken by the management, it tries to suppress them.

In the cooperative sector mill, the management does not have to play this role so intensively since its recruitment procedure is regulated by the Government's rules. The role of other influences in the matter is minimized. By playing leaders of unions against one another, the management of this mill seeks to break labour agitations and to browbeat them. Since there is already a strong caste line up in the workforce, the management does not have to fear the class crystallization.

The staff associations are not encouraged by the mill managements. The limited members in the staff organisation and their uninterest in association activities are mainly responsible for their less bargaining power. This is due to the fear that the management would take vengeful action against them. In the absence of any powerful unifying factors, caste remains to be the dominant interest of the staff.

Generally the unions in both the mills are infected by the spirit of caste. The vested interest and corruption of the union leaders disfavour the unity of workers. The working class solidarity is thus a casualty of the present position. Similarly, among the staff, there is no unity, some are willing to safeguard the interests of the management, and the others have differences with the management because of their recurring grievances. There is thus no class consciouness among them as "the middle management".

It is evident that caste loyalty has less role in the urban mill than in the rural mill. It may be surmised that in the course of time, this trend will create a situation in which caste relation will lose its importance in the urban mill. This will also perculate in the rural mill and create a similar situation there in future.

Bibliography

BOOKS

..ron, Raymond. *18 Lectures on Industrial Society*. Translated by M.K. Bottomore. London : Weidenfeld and Nicolson, 1961.

Baud, I.S.A. *Women's Labour in the Indian Textile Industry : The Influence of Technology and Organization on the Gender Division of Labour.* International Relations and Industrial Structures, Report No. 23. Tilburg : Tilburg University, 1983.

Rendix, Reinhard, and Lipset, S.M. eds. *Class, Status and Power*. London : Routledge and Kagan Paul, 1974.

Berreman, Gerald D. *Caste and Other Inequalities : Essays in Inequality*. Meerut : Folklore Institute, 1970.

Beteille, Andre. *Caste, Class and Power : Changing Patterns of Stratification in a Tanjore Village*. Berkeley : University of California Press, 1965.

———*Castes : Old and New*, Bombay : Asia, 1969.

———*Social Inequality*. Penguin Books, 1969.

———*Inequality among Men*. Oxford : Basil Blackwell, 1977.

———*The Idea of Natural Inequality and Other Essays*, Bombay : Oxford University Press, 1983.

Bhatt, Anil. *Caste, Class and Politics*. Delhi : Manohar, 1975.

Blau, Peter M, and Richard, Scott W. *Formal Organizations : A Comparative Approach.* London : Routledge and Kegan Paul, 1963.

Blunt, E.A.H. *The Caste System of Northern India.* London : Oxford University Press, 1931.

Bougle, Celeston. *Essays on Caste System.* Translated by D.F. Pocock. Cambridge : Cambridge University Press, 1971.

Chaudhuri, K.N. and Duwey, C.J. eds. *Economy and Society : Essays in Indian Economic and Social History.* Delhi : Oxford University Press, 1979.

Chaudhuri, M.R. *Indian Industries Development and Location.* Calcutta : Oxford University Press, 1970.

Cole, G.D.H. *Studies in Class Structure.* London : Routledge and Kegan Paul, 1955.

Crouch, Harold. *Trade Unions and Politics in India.* Bombay : Manaktalas, 1966.

Dahrendorf, Ralph. *Class and Class Conflict in Industrial Society.* London : Routledge and Kegan Paul 1959.

Davis, Keith. *Human Behaviour at Work : The Dynamics of Organisation Behaviour,* 3rd ed. New Delhi : Tata McGraw Hill, 1967.

Davis, Kingsley. *Human Society.* New York : Macmillan, 1965.

Dayal, Ishwar, and Sharma, Baldev R. *Management o; Trade Unions,* New Delhi : Sri Ram Centre for Industrial Relations and Human Resources, 1976.

D'Souza, Victor S. *Social Structure of a Planned City.* Bombay : Orient Longman, 1968.

———*Inequality and Its Perpetuation.* New Delhi : Manohar, 1981.

Duberman, Lucile. *Social Inequality : Class and Ca·te in America.* Philadelphia : J.B. Lippincott Co., 1976.

Dumont, Louis. *Homo Hierarchicus : The Caste System and Its Implications,* London : Weidenfeld and Nicolson, 1970.

Etzioni, Amitai. *Modern Organizations.* New Delhi : Prentice Hall, 1972.

Ghurye, G.S. *Caste and Race in India*. 5th ed. Bombay : Popular Prakashan, 1969.

Giri, V.V. *Labour Problems in Indian Industry*. Bombay : Asia, 1972.

Holmstorm, Mark. *South Indian Factory Workers : Their Life and Their World*. Bombay : Allied, 1978.

Hutton, J.H. *Caste in India*. 4th ed. Bombay : Oxford University Press, 1963.

Jayaraman, Raja. *Caste and Class : Dynamics of Inequality in Indian Society*. Delhi : Hindustan Publishing Corporation, 1981.

Karnik, V.D. *Indian Trade Unions : A Survey*. Bombay : Manaktalas, 1978.

Ketkar, S.V. *History of Caste in India*. Reprinted. Jaipur : Rawat, 1909.

Kolenda, Pauline. *Caste in Contemporary India : Beyond Organic Solidarity*, London : The Benjamin/Cummings Publishing Co., 1978.

Kothari, Rajni. *Caste in Indian Politics*. New Delhi : Orient Longman, 1970.

Kuthiala, S.K. *From Tradition to Modernity*. New Delhi : Abhinav Publications, 1973.

Lambert, Richard D. *Workers, Factories and Social Change in India*. Princeton, N.J. : Princeton University Press, 1963.

Leach, E.R. ed. *Aspects of Caste in South India, Ceylon and North-West Pakistan*. Cambridge : Cambridge University Press, 1962.

Lockwood, David. *The Blackcoated Worker : A Study in Class Conseiousness*. London : Unwin University Books, 1958.

Mahadevan, R. "Entrepreneurship and Business Communities in Colonial Madras, 1900-1920 : Some preliminary observations." In *Business Communities of India : A Historical Perspective*, edited by Dwijendra Tripathi. New Delhi : Manohar, 1984.

Mandelbaum, David G. *Society in India.* 2 Vols. Bombay : Popular Prakashan, 1972.

Marriott, Mckim, ed. *Village India : Studies in the Little Community.* Chicago : The University of Chicago Press, 1972.

Marx, Karl. *The Poverty of Philosophy.* Moscow : Progress Publishers, 1975.

Marx, Karl, and Engles, Frederick. *Selected Works.* Moscow : Progress Publishers, 1975.

Mathur, J.S. *Indian Working-Class Movement.* Allahabad : Central Book Depot, 1964.

Mayer, Adrin C. *Caste and Kinship in Central India.* Berkeley : University of California Press, 1960.

Mayer, Kurt and Buckly, Walter. *Class and Society.* 3rd ed. New York : Random House, 1970.

Mehrotra S.N. *Labour Problems in India.* New Delhi : S. Chand and Co., 1981.

Miller, Delbert C. and Form, William H. *Industrial Sociology : Work in Organizational Life.* 3rd ed. New York: Harper and Row, 1980.

Morris, Morris David. *The Emergence of an Industrial Labour Force in India : A Study of the Bombay Cotton Mills, 1854-1947.* Berkeley : University of California Press, 1965.

Mukerjee, Indrani. *Industrial Workers in a Developing Society : A Sociological Study,* Delhi : Mittal, 1985.

Mukerjee, Radhakamal. *The Indian Working Class.* Bombay : Hind Kitab Ltd., 1945.

Murphy, Eamn. *Unions in Conflicts : AComparative Study of Four South Indian Textile Centres, 1918-1939.* New Delhi : Manohar, 1981.

Myers, Charles A. *Industrial Relations in India.* Bombay : Asia, 1958.

———*Labour Problems in the Industrialization of India.* Cambridge, Massachusetts : Harvard University Press, 1958.

O'Malley. *Indian Caste Customs.* Cambridge : Cambridge University Press, 1932.

———*Indian's Social Heritage*, New Delhi : Vikas, 1976.

Pillai, Devadas S. *Men and Machines.* Bombay : Popular Prakashan, 1968.

Ramaswamy, E.A., and Ramaswamy, Uma. *Industry and Labour : An Introduction*, Delhi : Oxford University Press, 1981.

Ramaswamy, Uma. *Work, Union and Community.* Delhi : Oxford University Press, 1983.

Rudolph, Lloyd I., Rudolph Susanne H. *The Modernity of Tradition : Political Development in India.* Bombay : Orient Longman, 1967.

Saberwal, Satish. *Mobile Men ; Limits to Social Change in Urban Punjab*, New Delhi : Vikas, 1976.

Schneider, Eugene V. *Industrial Sociology.* New Delhi : Tata McGraw Hill, 1979.

Senart, Emile. *Caste in India : The Facts and the System.* Reprinted. New Delhi : Ess Ess Publications, 1975.

Sengupta, Syamal Kanti. *Caste Status Group Aggregate and Class.* Calcutta : Firma KLM, 1979.

Sharma, Baldev Raj. *The Indian Industrial Worker : Issues in Perspective.* Delhi : Vikas, 1974.

Sharma, K.L. *The Changing Rural Stratification : A Comparative Study of Six Villages in Rajasthan*, India. New Delhi: Orient Longman, 1974.

———*Essays in Social Stratification*, Jaipur : Rawat, 1980.

———*Caste, Class and Social Movement*, Jaipur : Rawat, 1986.

Sheth, N.R. *The Social Framework of Indian Factory.* Bombay : Oxford University Press, 1968.

Silverberg, James. ed. *Social Mobility in the Caste System in India.* The Hague : Mouton, 1968.

Singh, V.B. *Labour Research in India.* Bombay : Popular Prakashan, 1970.

Singh, Yogendra. *Modernization of Indian Tradition : A Systematic Study of Social Change*. Reprinted. Jaipur : Ratwat, 1986.

Somalay, *Madurai Maavattam.* Vedaraniam : K.G.K.G. Publication, 1980.

Sood, Santosh. *Trade Union Leadership in India: A Case Study.* New Delhi : Deep and Deep, 1984.

Srinivas, M.N. *Social Change in Modern India.* Bombay, Allied, 1966.

Srinivas, M.N., Seshaiah, S. ; and Parthasarthy, V.S. eds. *Dimensions of Social Change.* Bombay : Allied, 1977.

Swingewood, Alan. *Marx and Modern Social Theory.* London : Macmillan, 1975.

Thurston, Edgar, *Caste and Tribes of Southern India.* 7 vols. Madras : Government Press, 1909.

Tumin, Melvin M. *Social Stratification.* New Delhi : Prentice Hall, 1969.

Vaid, K.N. *Contract Labour in Manufacturing Industries : A Report and An Analysis.* New Delhi : Shri Ram Centre Press, 1966.

———*Gheraos and Labour Unrest in West Bengal.* New Delhi: Sri Ram Centre for Industrial Relations and Human: Resources, 1972.

Verma, K.K. *Changing Role of Caste Associations.* New Delhi National Publishing House, 1979.

Weber, Max. *From Max Weber : Essays in Sociology.* Translated and edited by H.H. Gerth and C.W. Mills. Reprinted. London : Routledge and Kegan Paul, 1977.

JOURNAL ARTICLES

Ames, Michael M. "Modernization and Social Structure : Family, Caste and Class in Jamshedpur," *Economic and Political Weekly* 4 (July 1969) : 1217-1224.

Anant, Santokh Singh. "Caste-Hindu Attitudes : The Harijans' Perception." *Asian Survey* 11 (March 1971) : 271-278.

Armstrong, Peter. "Class Relationship at the Point of Production : A Case Study." *Sociology : The Journal of the British Sociological Association* 17 (August 1983) : 339-358.

Arya, P. Prakash. "Workers' Involvement in Trade Unions." *Indian Journal of Labour Economics* 23 (October 1980) : 115-131.

Bailey, F.G. "Closed Social Stratification in India." *European Journal of Sociology* 4 (1963) : 107-124.

Bhatt, Bhal J. "The Changing Characteristics of the Indian Industrial Workforce." *Indian Journal of Industrial Relations* 11 (October 1975) : 143-160.

Chattopadhyaya, G., and Sengupta, A.K. "Growth of a Disciplined Labour Force : A Case Study of Social Impediments." *Economic and Political Weekly* 4 (July 1959) : 1209-1216.

Child, John., Pearce, Sandra' and King, Losa. "Class Perception and Social Identification of Industrial Supervisors." *Sociology : The Journal of the British Sociological Association* 14 (August 1980) : 363-399.

Cox, Oliver C. "Race and Caste : A Distinction." *American Journal of Sociology* 50 (March 1945) : 360-368.

Davis, Kingsley, and Moore, Wilbert E. "Some Principles of Stratification." *American Sociological Review* 10 (1945) : 242-249.

Dodge, Cole P., and Weibe, Paul D. "Tamil Repatriates in Madurai : Problems and Prospects." *Economic and Political Weekly* 16 (January 1981) : 159-162.

Dos Santos, Theotonio. "The Concept of Social Class." *Science and Society*. Translated by Henry F. Mins. 34 (1970) : 166-193.

Greatz, Brian R. "Images of Class in Modern Society : Structure, Sentiment and Social Location." *Sociology : The Journal of the British Sociological Association* 17 (February 1983) ; 79-96.

Goil, R.M. "White Collar Unionism in India with Special Reference to Madhya Pradesh." *The Indian Journal of Labour Economics* 10 (January 1968) : C-107-C-121.

Goldthorpe, John H. "Social Stratification in Industrial Society." *Sociological Review* 8 (April 1964) : 97-139.

Gupta, Dipankar. "Caste, Infrastructure and Superstructure : A Critique." *Economic and Political Weekly* 16 (December 1981) : 2093-2104.

Hardgrove (Jr.), Robert L. "Caste : Fission and Fusion." *Economic and Political Weekly* 3 (1968) :1065-1073.

Holmstorm, Mark, "Caste and Status in an Indian City." *Economic and Political Weekly* 7 (April 1972) : 769-774.

Jones, Bryn. "Max Weber and The Concept of Social Class." *The Sociological Review* n.s. (November 1975) : 729-757.

Joshi, Chitra. "Kanpur Textile Labour : Some Structural Features of Formative Years." *Economic and Political Weekly* 16 (November 1981) : 1823-1838.

Kiuranov, Chavdar. "Social Classes and Social Stratification." *International Journal of Sociology* 12 (Fall 1982) : 5-30.

Landecker, Werner S. "Class Crystallization and Class Consciousness." *American Sociological Review* 28 (April 1963) : 219-228.

Lieten, George Kristoffel. "Caste in Class Politics." *Economic and Political Weekly* 14 (February 1979) : 313-328.

Madan, T.N. "Caste and Development." *Economic and Political Weekly* 4 (February 1969) : 285-290.

Mamkottam, K. "Factionalism and Power in Trade unions : A Case Study." *Indian Journal of Industrial Relations* 13 (October 1977), 167-190.

Meillassoux, Claude, "Are there Castes in India?" *Economy and Society* 2 (1973) : 89-111.

Murphy, E.D. "Class and Community in India : The Madras Labour Union, 1918-1921." *The Indian Economic and Social History Review* 14 (July-September 1977) : 291-321.

Nichols, Theo. "Labourism and Class Consciousness : The 'Class Ideology' of some Northern Foremen." *Thc Sociological Review* 22 (November 1974) : 483-502.

Pandit, Nalini. "Caste and Class in Maharashtra." *Economic and Political Weekly* Annual number (February 1979) : 425-436.

Pillai, Aijayan Kumara, "Dimensions of Caste in India." *International Review of Modern Sociology* 12 (Autumn 1982) : 229-235.

Platt, Jennifer. "Variations in Answers to Different Questions on Perception of Class." *Sociological Review* 19 (August 1971) : 409-419.

Pocok, David F. "Sociologies : Urban and Rural." *Contributions to Indian Sociology* 4 (1969) : 63-81.

Ponday, Rajendra. "Continuity and Change in Caste System in Rural India." *Social Change* 13 (September 1983) : 3-7.

———"Karl Marx's Theory of Class and Contemporary Marxist Conceptualization." *The Journal of Sociological Studies* 3 (January 1984) : 127-141.

Ramaswamy, E.A. "Trade Unionism and Caste in South India." *Modern Asian Studies* 10 (1976) : 361-373.

Robinson, Robert V. "Explaining Perceptions of Class and Racial Inequality in England and the United States of America." *British Journal of Sociology* 34 (September 1983): 344-366.

Sengupta, Anil, K. "Trade Unions, Politics and the State : A Case from West Bengal." *Contributions to Indian Sociology* (January-June 1977) : 45-68.

Sharma, Baldev Raj. "The Industrial Worker : Some Myths and Realities." *Economic and Political Weekly* 5 (May 1970) : 875-878.

———"The Indian Industrial Worker : His Origin, Experience and Destiny." *Economic and Political Weekly* 8 (June 1973) : M-38-M-48.

Sheth, N.R. "Society and Industrial Work in India." *Human Organization* 26 (Spring/Summer 1967) : 77-89.

———"Sociological Studies of Indian Industrial Workers." *Sociological Bulletin* 26 (March 1977) : 76-90.

———"Trade Unions in India : A Sociological Approach." *Sociological Bulletin* 17 (March 1968) : 5-18.

———"Workers' Participation in Trade Union Activity." *Indian Journal of Industrial Relations* 4 (January 1969) ; 279-298.

Sheth, N.R. and Jain, S.P. "Workers, Leaders and Politics : A Case Study." *Indian Journal of Industrial Relations* 3 (January 1968) : 286-289.

Singh, Jaspal. "Social Background of Trade Union Leaders." *Economic and Political Weekly* 34 (August 1970): 1421-1424.

Singh, Sri Narain. "Rural Factory Workers : An Attitudinal Study." *Social Change* 13 (September 1983) : 31-33

Sinha, Ramesh P. "Workers, Participation in Unions and Participation Correlates." *Indian Journal of Industrial Relations* 19 (July 1983) : 45-56.

Srinivas, M.N. "Social Environment and Management's Responsibilities." *Economic and Political Weekly* 10 (March 1975) : 487-491.

Srivastawa, Vinita. "Changing Facets of Indian Factory Workers." *Indian Journal of Social Work* 41 (October 1980) : 309-318.

Stern, Henri. "Power in Modern India : Caste or Class? : An Approach and Case Study." *Contributions to Indian Sociology* 13 (1979) : 61-83.

Vaid, K.N. "Why Workers join Unions?" *Indian Journal of Industrial Relations* 1 (1965) : 208-230.

Wright, E.O., Costello, C., Hachin, D., and Sprague, J. "The American Class Structure." *American Sociological Review* 47 (December 198) : 709-726.

CENSUS

Census of India, 1961.

Censes of India (Primary Census Abstract), 1981.

GAZETTEER

Gazetteer of India : Tamil Nadu (Ramanathapuram District), 1972.

PROJECT

Ramachandra Raj G. *In the Context of Conflict in the Larger System : A Study of Industrial Conflict in Kerala.* New Delhi : Project financed by Indian Council of Social Science Research, 1976.

REPORT

Royal Commission on Labour in India. *The Report, Royal Commission on Labour.* Calcutta, 1931.

SURVEY

Indian Council of Social Science Research. *A Survey oj Research in Sociology and Social Anthropolagy*, Vol. 1. New Delhi : Indian Council of Social Science Research, 1974.

Indian Council of Social Science Research. *A Survey of Research in Sociology and Social Anthropology*, Vol. 2. New Delhi : Indian Council of Social Science Research, 1985.

Index